THE NEW WORKER
IN SOVIET RUSSIA

RUSSIA OLD AND NEW SERIES
Jules Koslow, General Editor

THE NEW WORKER IN SOVIET RUSSIA

IRVING R. LEVINE

The Macmillan Company, New York, New York
Collier Macmillan Publishers, London

The Macmillan Company
866 Third Avenue, New York, N.Y. 10022
Collier-Macmillan Canada Ltd., Toronto, Ontario

Library of Congress Catalog Card Number:
72–92451

First Printing

Printed in the United States of America

*Dedicated with love
to Nancy, Jeffrey, Daniel,
and Jennifer*

Acknowledgments

My first exposure to the toils and troubles of Russian workers came as a child. My father Joseph Levine, who had been born near Kiev, related his youthful experiences when, out of sympathy for those oppressed by the czarist government, he joined other young intellectuals in underground activities against the authorities. Acting as a courier to deliver anticzarist pamphlets in the period leading up to the 1905 revolution, he was arrested and exiled to Siberia. His subsequent escape from the country was briefly placed in jeopardy; stopped near the border, he momentarily could not bring to mind the name on the forged passport he was carrying.

Years later, as NBC News correspondent in the Soviet Union, I witnessed the vastly changed, but still burdensome, conditions of Russian workers under a Communist state.

This book draws also from the vast literature that has accumulated on the Russian worker through the ages. As John Milton put it in his *Brief History of Muscovia:* "What was scatter'd in many volumes, and observ'd at several times by Eye-witnesses, with no cursory pains I laid together, to save the Reader a far longer travaile. . . ."

For their indispensable contributions to this "travaile," I must thank —besides my father, for initiating my early interest in the subject, and my wife Nancy, for her encouragement and help—the authors past and present whose writings provided source material.

I also want to express thanks to Jules Koslow, editor of the Russia Old and New Series, for enlisting me in this project, and to Kathie Fried, my talented editor at The Macmillan Company, for her patience and guidance. To Jane Swanson in Rome, where the book was begun, and to Dorothy Buckner in Washington, where it was completed, my appreciation for their work in preparing the manuscript.

Irving R. Levine
WASHINGTON, D.C.
DECEMBER 3, 1972

Contents

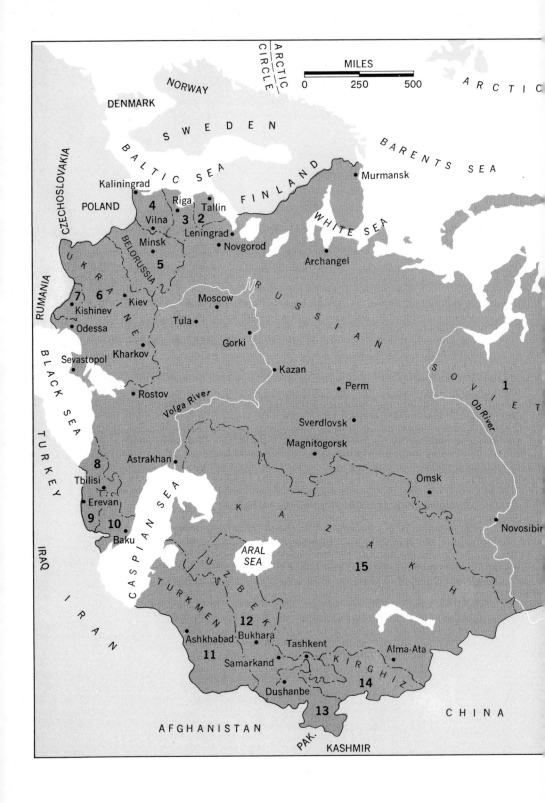

MILES

0   250   500

NORWAY

DENMARK

CZECHOSLOVAKIA

POLAND

Kaliningrad

Riga

Vilna

Tallin

Leningrad

Minsk

Novgorod

Murmansk

ARCTIC CIRCLE

ARCTIC

SWEDEN

BALTIC SEA

FINLAND

BARENTS SEA

WHITE SEA

Archangel

RUMANIA

UKRAINE

BELORUSSIA

Kishinev

Kiev

Odessa

Kharkov

Moscow

Tula

Gorki

R U S S I A N

Kazan

Perm

S O V I E T

Ob River

BLACK SEA

Sevastopol

Rostov

Volga River

Sverdlovsk

TURKEY

Astrakhan

Magnitogorsk

Omsk

Tbilisi

Erevan

Baku

CASPIAN SEA

K   A   Z   A   K   H

Novosibir

IRAQ

IRAN

TURKMEN

UZBE

ARAL SEA

15

Ashkhabad

Bukhara

Samarkand

Tashkent

Alma-Ata

Dushanbe

KIRGHIZ

AFGHANISTAN

PAK.

KASHMIR

CHINA

4

3

2

5

7

6

8

9

10

12

11

13

14

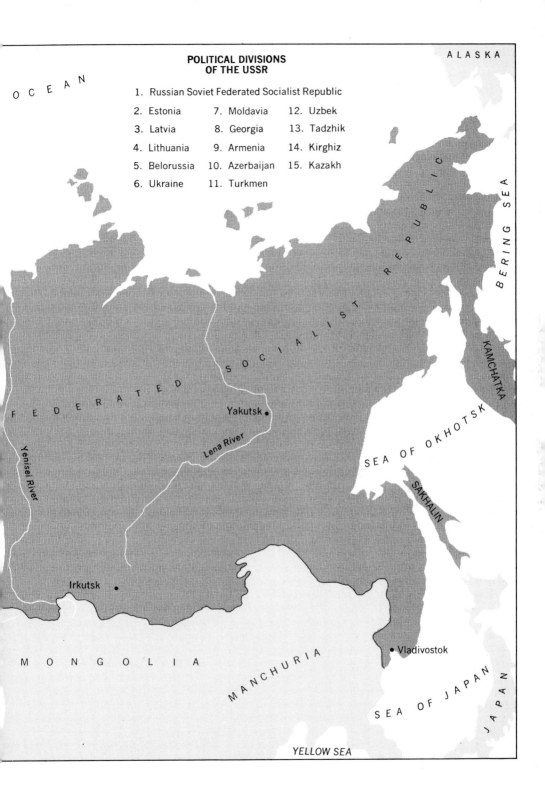

POLITICAL DIVISIONS
OF THE USSR

1. Russian Soviet Federated Socialist Republic

2. Estonia	7. Moldavia	12. Uzbek
3. Latvia	8. Georgia	13. Tadzhik
4. Lithuania	9. Armenia	14. Kirghiz
5. Belorussia	10. Azerbaijan	15. Kazakh
6. Ukraine	11. Turkmen	

ALASKA

OCEAN

BERING SEA

RUSSIAN SOVIET FEDERATED SOCIALIST REPUBLIC

KAMCHATKA

SEA OF OKHOTSK

SAKHALIN

Yenisei River

Lena River

Yakutsk

Irkutsk

MONGOLIA

MANCHURIA

Vladivostok

SEA OF JAPAN

JAPAN

YELLOW SEA

1 The First Workers and Peter the Great, 1682-1725

THE story of the Russian worker must begin with the story of an incredible ruler, Czar Peter I, known as Peter the Great. The nonagricultural worker became important in Russia only with the growth of industry, and the first industry of any importance in that vast country began with Peter.

The first Russian workers, in their misery, were the creation of this relentless man. Peter was obsessed with the idea of converting the economy of his backward, agricultural country into an industrial one. In pursuit of this ambition, he exacted cruel sacrifices from the Russian masses. There was no gradual transition from peasant farmer to factory worker. People were uprooted from their homes and from their accustomed life of working the land and were impressed into service at primitive machines.

The history of the Russian worker not only *starts* with Peter the Great, but, in a sense, the shadow of this unique czar is cast over the entire history of the Russian worker.

Peter the Great's driving passion was to modernize the backward, mainly agricultural country he had inherited and make it European rather than Asian in thinking and technology. To accomplish this, he considered it essential to improve his large army and build a navy. These would enable him to hold his own against the superior civilizations of Europe and to establish a footing on the Baltic Sea for his country, which, for all practical purposes, was both land- and ice-locked. It was only by sea that Russia could have direct contact with Western Europe, its commerce, and its knowledge so necessary for helping Russia to become a modern, industrial state.

It was clear to Peter that a country's military power depended very much on the quality and productive capacity of her industries. Under Peter, factories of many types grew rapidly. He recruited a large number of experts from foreign lands to build and run the factories; throughout Europe, Russian embassies acted as employment agencies to hire the needed technicians lacking in Russia.

An industrialized state requires a great deal more than factory buildings and technicians. It requires efficient organization and administration of people and products. A national cohesion and discipline are needed too. Russia lacked all of these. Peter set about with almost superhuman resoluteness to metamorphize Russia. As absolute ruler of his country, Peter could use human life and natural resources as he wished; he had no one to answer to for his actions, however rash or ruthless they might be. Among the principal victims were the workers.

The Russian worker of Peter the Great's time—and for a long time following—was exploited and oppressed, ignorant and poor. The village or town in which he lived consisted of low, mean houses, often with thatched roofs. The houses were protected against the cold by plastering inside and out with mud. The stoves were made of brick and burned mainly wood.

The streets of the community were unpaved and ankle-deep in dust in summer and knee-deep in mud in spring. Sometimes there were wooden trottoirs, slightly elevated wooden sidewalks to prevent booted feet from becoming mired in mud.

In one corner of the Russian worker's hovel there was almost certain to hang a small, crude icon—an image of Christ or a saint. Sometimes a tiny oil flame flickered beneath it. The Russian

Czar Peter I. *Tass from Sovfoto*

worker, like other Russians, was apt to be very religious and, more likely than not, regularly attended the Russian Orthodox Church. His religion was less a matter of conviction than of a multitude of superstitions. He believed in strange stories of vampires and devils as firmly as in the Gospel. There were a great variety of devils—

house devils, forest devils, stable devils, factory and workshop devils. For each of these there was some special antidote. For instance, if the Russian owned a horse, he would keep a goat in the stable because goats were thought to keep the stable devil from injuring the horse. When a Russian worker yawned, he made the sign of the cross in front of his mouth before closing it to prevent the devil from entering. Russian priests were believed to be exorcists—that is, to have the power to drive away evil spirits.

Vodka, the colorless Russian alcoholic drink, distilled from potatoes or barley, was often made at home and was available at low prices in stores. As might be expected, drunkenness was prevalent. The Russian worker's diet consisted mainly of black bread and a kind of porridge or mush made from coarse cracked buckwheat or barley and known as *kasha*. The traditional beverage was hot tea, always drunk from a glass. If he used a knife and fork on the rare occasions when he ate meat, the knife and fork would go alternately to his mouth. In fact, table knives of Russian manufacture, or made elsewhere for Russian use, were always fashioned with a large, broad end, the better to deliver food from plate to mouth.

The worker's manners were crude. Handkerchiefs were almost unknown—he blew his nose with his fingers. Men and women wore colorless clothing of coarse, stiff, durable material. There were no schools for the Russian worker or his children, and illiteracy was almost universal among members of the working class.

Working conditions were cruel and primitive. A military atmosphere prevailed in early industrial enterprises. Promotions were made to various grades and ranks as in the army. Persons who violated work rules were tried by tribunals that resembled courtsmartial.

A special commission was appointed by the state, in the last year of Peter's reign, to look into the poor quality of manufactured goods. It attributed shortcomings in part to "the very bad buildings in which work was being done; the lighting was inadequate and the roofs leaked . . . in the majority of undertakings there were no covered floors . . . there were no stone, brick, or wooden floors. The workers were badly dressed and few of them had a whole shirt on their backs."

The first set of government regulations concerning working conditions was issued in 1722. It is rather shocking to note that the same set of regulations remained in force for over a century and a quarter—until 1853—so slow were Russia's leaders to change and reform. The regulations of 1722 fixed the working day at ten hours in the winter months and thirteen hours in the summer. In winter, from September 10 to March 10, a bell summoned the people to work one hour before sunrise and tolled again to dismiss them one hour after sunset. There were 250 working days in the year. The remaining 115 days were Sundays, religious and state feast days, and free days. The free days—numbering about thirty a year—were intended to enable peasants employed in factories to work their own land.

The first decree regulating wages was promulgated by Peter the Great in 1724. The decree seemed to equate the value of a horse with that of a man. It fixed the rates of pay for work done in the mines "by men and horses" at "ten kopecks per day in summer for a peasant and a horse, and five kopecks per day for a peasant without a horse; in winter, six and four respectively." The decree applied only to unskilled workers; skilled workers and foreign workers received higher wages. As Russians acquired industrial skills themselves, the differential in wages between Russians and foreign experts diminished. The wages paid unskilled workers remained at practically the same level for almost fifty years. A chart gives the wage rates paid in state factories in the Ural province in the eighteenth century:[1]

	Rubles per year		
	1723	*1737*	*1766*
Foreign foreman	100	36	36
Russian foreman	24–36	30–36	36
Journeyman	15–24	15–24	24
Apprentice and unskilled laborer	12–18	10–15	12–18

(A man would have had to earn about 30 rubles a year to provide himself and his family with bare necessities.)

Peasants attached to factories and mines were able to stay alive despite the low wages because of the practice that allowed them to

1. K. Pazhitnov, *Hours of Work in the Mining Industry* (St. Petersburg, 1906).

spend some time working in their own small plots of land, raising crops and perhaps an animal or two.

The workers were required to buy food they did not raise themselves at company stores, where prices were often higher than in the marketplace; and the charges were deducted from their wages. In most cases factories were built some distance from villages and trading centers, especially in the Ural Mountains and in Siberia, so that the stores were a necessity. A government rule issued in 1735 pertaining to the sale of provisions at factory stores prescribed that "the quality must be good, weights and measures correct, and prices must not exceed cost price plus 10 to 20 percent to cover overhead charges." The regulation was not always observed, and many workers never saw their wages in actual cash after deductions for store purchases and for taxes had been made.

An indication of the abuses suffered by workers is seen in a decree issued by Peter the Great in 1736. It stated that punishment of workers by flogging could be carried out only in the presence of all the workers of a factory or of all the inhabitants of a village. Cruel as this may seem, Peter's decree was intended as a reform! Its purpose was to prevent floggings in private. By requiring that such beatings could be carried out only in public, a form of restraint was imposed on factory managers.

Peter the Great was a man whose character and accomplishments—whose very physical appearance—boggle the mind. Six feet nine inches tall, Peter stood above any crowd and was enormously strong—he could bend a silver coin in his hands. He liked to boast that he was a dentist, astronomer, engraver, cannonmaker, sailor, bootmaker, shipbuilder, and the master of eight other trades; and it was no empty boast. He was acknowledged to be the best ship's carpenter in all Russia. In the Kremlin Museum today you can see a fine pair of boots that he made for himself and wore; they come to the waist of an ordinary man.

Everything about him was bigger than life-size. He has been likened to a moving thunderbolt because of his ceaseless activity, the power of his personality, and his utter lack of restraint. His vices were many: he would drink himself into a stupor with a group of companions (but he was capable of rallying quickly), he had atrocious manners, and a terrible capacity for cruelty. On the other hand, he had inexhaustible energy and curiosity, steadfastness of purpose, and a quick and lively, if not deep, intelligence. And Peter placed the greatness and prestige of Russia above all other considerations.

Before the reign of Peter I, Russia was an isolated Asian country in relation to Europe. After his death in 1725, Russia ranked among the major powers of Europe. He accomplished the first of Russia's revolutions. The second occurred two centuries later. This was the Bolshevik Revolution, which we will discuss in Chapter 6.

Peter's efforts to create a new Russian civilization touched every human activity. He brought out the first textbook on social behavior in which "his subjects were ordered to be amiable, modest, and respectful, to learn languages, to look people in the face, take off their hats, not to dance in boots, or to spit on the floor, or sing too loud, put the finger in the nose, rub the lips with the hand, lean on the table, swing the legs, lick the fingers, gnaw a bone when at dinner, scratch one's head, talk with one's mouth full."[2] Peter also personally simplified the Russian alphabet and became the editor of the first public newspaper in the land. He ordered the translation into Russian of a great number of books on every imaginable subject.

In foreign eyes the waist-long beards worn in Russia were considered symbols of a medieval and barbarian society. Peter personally cut off the beards of five of his principal nobles and ordered that no one should come into his presence unshaven. So great was the opposition in the country that Peter was obliged to exempt persons outside the court upon payment of a tax for a beard license.

He also tried to change the sleeping habits of the nobles by announcing to both the gentlemen *and* ladies of the court that anyone caught sleeping with boots on would be instantly de-

2. Sir Bernard Pares, *A History of Russia* (New York: Alfred A. Knopf, 1926), p. 225.

capitated. Russians were ordered to wear Western dress instead of cumbersome, long-skirted robes.

Peter changed Russia's calendar, built the country's first modern hospitals and medical schools, and prescribed the construction of stone houses and the establishment of fire departments to put an end to the disastrous conflagrations of the wooden cities. A system of taxation was instituted; instead of the single tax on land, a great variety of excise taxes was imposed (on births, marriages, baths, stovepipes, horse troughs, cucumbers, and coffins). Peter ordered the country's first census. He also is said to have introduced tobacco and smoking into Russia. Education was made compulsory for children of the gentry, the upper or ruling class; the curriculum was reading, writing, arithmetic, geometry, and fortification.

Under Peter the Great many young Russians were sent abroad to study so that their knowledge could be used for supervising workers in the budding industries. Peter himself was the first czar to leave Russia. Many of Peter's reforms followed his grand tour of Europe at the age of twenty-four. The trip lasted for a year and a half, and he tried to travel incognito. It was a little difficult, however, not to attract attention since he moved about with a retinue of 250 people, including dwarfs and jesters. He took the pseudonym of Peter Mikhailov and attached himself to a Russian diplomatic mission that traveled to European capitals seeking an alliance against Turkey.

Peter's real object was to study Europe and to recruit teachers of the many skills that his country lacked. He visited Germany, France, Denmark, England, and Austria. In Holland alone he enlisted more than one thousand experts in various fields to come and work in Russia. From his European travels he also brought back dental instruments, including a pair of pliers; and he terrified courtiers in his eagerness to display his skill by wrenching teeth from their jaws. He proudly kept the teeth he had extracted in a little bag.

To symbolize his country's turning toward the developed West, Peter built a new capital to replace Moscow, which is deep in the interior of Russia's vast territory. The site of the new city was on the Baltic Sea, much of whose coastline he had wrested from

Sweden in twelve years of war (actually, during Peter's long reign Russia was at peace for only two years). Named St. Petersburg, it was Russia's "window on Europe." It was characteristic of Peter's method of total concentration on an objective that he ordered that no stone house be built anywhere in Russia until a certain number had been completed in his new capital. In this way all of the nation's construction resources were focused on the task.

Peter's herculean efforts succeeded in building "a heavy industry, which in the end supplied all the ordnance requirements both of his army and his navy; a rope, sail, and lumber industry, which met all the needs of his navy; and a cloth industry, which furnished uniforms for a large proportion of his troops."[3]

By the time of Peter's death, Russian production of pig iron was probably larger than that of England—regarded as the home of the industrial revolution. In 1718 Russia was smelting thirty thousand tons of pig iron, whereas England only reached two-thirds of this figure in 1740. As a result of the beginnings made under Peter, Russia had become the world's largest producer of iron and copper by the middle of the 1700s.

Of the 195 largest factories established during Peter's reign, twenty produced iron and other metal products; twenty-six manufactured linen, silk fabrics, and other textiles; five made leather; four, paper; and three, weapons. Some of these plants employed well over a thousand workers each; and others, several hundred. However, not all were centralized plants in the present-day sense, with workers tending machinery in a single building. In some cases, the various works of the unit were carried out in separated workrooms as well as by hundreds of domestic workers, each in his own home; the factory management coordinated their activities. This tended to be the pattern, particularly in weaving and other branches of textile manufacturing.

The very nature of production in the metallurgical industry required the concentration of large numbers of workers under a single roof. These establishments bore some resemblance to fac-

3. B. H. Sumner, *Peter the Great and the Emergence of Russia* (New York: The Macmillan Company, 1951).

tories in the modern sense, with considerable division of labor, and machinery run by water power.

The reign of Peter, so fundamental to the development of the Russian worker, lasted for forty-three years. He came to the throne at the age of ten, although he did not assume sole and complete power until he was seventeen. During the last four years of his life, he gave himself the title of emperor; the titles "czar" and "emperor" are used interchangeably (the word "czar" comes from the Latin *caesar*).

Peter died at the age of fifty-three. After a lifetime of physical excesses, he never recuperated from a chill caught while attempting to save some drowning sailors, whose boat had capsized in the Neva River.

For all that was evil in it, Peter the Great's period of power was one of the most fruitful epochs for Russia. Even the Communists, who hold small love or respect for any of the czars, regard Peter as a "progressive" and recount his achievements with an obvious measure of respect. An aristocrat of Peter's time, Prince M. Shcherbatov, was to write later that if Peter had not *bullied* Russia into civilization, the work that he did would have taken a hundred years or more.

2 The Serf Workers and the Czars, 1725–1855

ONE important thing was *not* changed by Peter. In the country of twelve million people, most were serfs at the end of Peter's reign as they had been at the beginning.

In theory, there was a difference between a serf and a slave. Unlike slaves, serfs were free to enter into contracts to buy or sell property; they were free to lend money, to trade, and to acquire land. But these were purely theoretical rights that had little or no meaning in practice. In actual fact, their property, if any, was at the mercy of their masters, the land-owning gentry; and, more and more, so were their very lives. In time, Russian serfs became slaves as indisputably as were the American Negroes before the Civil War.

The serfs' condition remained as bad under Peter as before and in some ways became worse. For their new factories, Peter and his successors needed workers quickly and in large numbers. These were obtainable in an agricultural country such as Russia only from among the peasants, the serf tillers of the soil. Peter recognized serfdom as something he could not replace: without serfs he

11

would have no labor force; and without labor, no instant industry.

The method of setting up a state factory was uncomplicated and direct. The czar would form a company by picking individuals, Russians or foreigners, to manage the enterprise. He would grant them an outright subsidy in addition to a government loan. They were exempted from taxation for a number of years. Most important, they were supplied with free labor by the simple expedient of making them absolute masters of all the serfs in a given area.

Members of the merchant class could become owners of factories and were permitted to buy entire village populations. The serf inhabitants could not be diverted to any other work. Such plants were called "possessional" factories—the serfs were as much the owner's possession as was the primitive machinery.

Besides state and possessional factories, there was a third type of factory. This was the so-called manorial factory, derived from the word "manor," which means "the house of a lord and the land belonging to it." Manorial factories were the property of landowners and were operated on their estates by serfs belonging to them.

Serfs too were the source of labor for mines and public works, such as the building of roads, bridges, and, of course, the city of St. Petersburg.

> It was the building of Peter's city which made the cruellest demands upon his subjects. Peter could not wait to see his dream of paradise realized. From every part of Russia he recruited droves of workers who, herded like cattle, labored almost with bare hands to clear the island stretches of swamp on which the city was raised. In conditions that bred recurring epidemics, tens of thousands of lives were sacrificed to his prodigal haste.[1]

It is difficult to visualize the conditions of servitude in eighteenth-century Russia. The peasants who were wrenched from the land and converted into industrial and manual workers had no say in the matter. They were not consulted. They were at the total and absolute disposal of their proprietors. Serfs were traded or freely

1. R. D. Charques, *A Short History of Russia* (New York: E. P. Dutton, 1956), p. 116.

given as gifts. They were used as payment for debts. If a noble killed someone else's serf, the law's main requirement was that he replace him with "one of the best" of his own serfs with family.

The serf was nothing more nor less than chattel, an item of transportable, tangible property. St. Petersburg newspapers of around 1750 contained advertisements of serfs for sale, especially girls.

The code of criminal law promulgated in 1754 granted the privileged classes "full power without exception" over the serfs; only torture and manslaughter were forbidden.

Virtually captive workers formed the major portion of Russia's industrial labor force for more than a century and a quarter after Peter the Great. However, during all of that period and longer, the worker in industry comprised a minority sector of the Russian population; the major part of the population consisted of peasants who worked the land.

In 1800, for example, Russia had a total population of about 36 million, the largest of any state in Europe. Of these, no more than 125,000 people could be classified as factory workers. By contrast, it is estimated that 34 million were peasants, of whom nearly 20 million were serfs on private estates; the remainder, state or crown peasants, were not far removed from the strict condition of serfdom. Even with the steady growth of industry (and of population), there were only a half million factory workers in 1855.

These statistics underscore the fact that, numerically at least, the chief victims of Russian serfdom were the peasants, not the workers. For a very long period in Russian history, the pressures for reform and the periodic uprisings against czarist tyranny originated in the sufferings of the peasants. The workers were too few, by comparison, really to matter.

Despite the flogging and worse that befell a serf caught fleeing from the land or enterprise to which he was assigned, thousands left. It has been estimated that from 1719 to 1727 no fewer than one hundred thousand serfs ran away. Some collected in large robber bands, others hid in the woods living like animals for as long as they could, and there were those who managed to get out of the country. Many joined a kind of foreign legion, the Cossacks, a favored military caste of border guards who had settlements in remote regions of Russia.

Besides the serfs, a second source of workers for Russia's new industries and construction projects were convicts. In addition, vagrants, dissolute women, and illegitimate children were sent to factories.

Thirdly, there was a small body of free workers, but they did not remain completely free for long. These were a relatively few artisans, handicraft workers, shopkeepers and other tradespeople, children of soldiers, and beggars. They were free to seek jobs in the new enterprises as they wished, negotiating their wages according to their intelligence and skills. However, in 1736, eleven years after Peter's death, a decree declared that all freemen working in factories, together with their families, must remain attached to their particular factory "forever" unless released by those in charge.

Low wages, unbearable working conditions, high prices at factory stores, corrupt managers, and physical punishment caused Russian workers on numerous occasions to turn violently against their employers and seize their factories. One fairly typical case occurred at a metal works in the town of Lipetsk. About thirteen hundred peasants were attached to the factory, which originally had been established by the state and in 1754 was handed over to a Prince Repnin. Under his management, the conditions of work deteriorated, and the workers asked the government to put the factory back under its control.

The workers' petition stated that their wages had been reduced by Prince Repnin to two and three kopecks a day, whereas previously it had been four to five kopecks. Instead of being paid in cash, they now received payments in goods. The petition complained that these goods were "scythes, knives, mittens, wax, incense, and horses," of such high price that they could not be resold or bartered.[2]

The workers further complained that they were forced to pay taxes twice, once to the factory management and once to the prince himself. The management got rid of troublesome workers

2. S. P. Turin, *From Peter the Great to Lenin* (London: Frank Cass & Co., 1968), p. 10.

by sending them to army recruiting offices; under state control, the workers had been exempt from hated military service.

The petition was delivered by a workers' representative named Kuprianov. A special unit of soldiers was dispatched to the plant to seize Kuprianov and flog him before his assembled comrades.

The infuriated workers attacked the soldiers and managed to set Kuprianov free. The workers then set up their own management for the factory and elected Kuprianov chairman. This state of affairs did not last long before the authorities regained control.

In 1760 when the workers in a plant owned by Kikita Demidov in the Ural Mountains staged an uprising against the management, troops carted 300 workers off to prison. Workers in the same factory claimed in a petition submitted to the government that between the years 1757 and 1760 no fewer than 328 workers had been flogged; one of the beaten workers had died and others were permanently maimed.

In addition to the uprisings, there were instances of a unique type of Russian strike. The workers did not simply stay away from their jobs, but rather they left the factory en masse, together with their families, and made their way back to their native villages, often hundreds of miles distant.

Workers of one factory deserting in this fashion composed a

Workers' strikes and uprisings were common even in the 1700s. Here strikers are violently dispersed by Cossacks. *Sovfoto*

warning for the government: "If we are hunted down and forcibly sent to the factories, there will be bloodshed on both sides and we therefore warn you of this, and are sending this warning everywhere, so that we may not be held responsible for any bloodshed which may occur."[3] The czar's government did not shrink from bloodshed.

We mentioned earlier that in 1718 Russia's output of pig iron far surpassed England's. This was in the early years of Russia's industrial development under Peter the Great. During the first half of the 1800s there was an almost explosive increase of industrial production elsewhere in Europe as new techniques were perfected. Russia's economic development was appreciable, too, but it lagged behind that of the rest of Europe.

For example—and still using pig iron as our yardstick—by 1800 England had caught up with Russia's production. By the 1850s Russia's output was far from being doubled, whereas England's had increased more than ten times. By 1860, Russia stood in eighth place among pig iron producers, behind even such small countries as Austria and Prussia.

There were a number of reasons for the widening gap between Russian industrial growth and that of other countries of Europe. For one thing, unfree workers are less productive than free workers. For another, since the majority of the Russian people were downtrodden, poverty-stricken, fettered peasants, mass markets existed for only a few commodities; relatively few people had money to buy more than the barest necessities.

Part of the explanation is found, too, in the character of Peter's successors. Several were endowed with great intelligence and personal force, but none matched the organizing ability, vision, will power, and dedication Peter had brought to the founding of Russian industry. They all shared his capacity for oppression in greater or lesser degree. It has been said that the Russian type of autocracy (a form of government in which one person possesses unlimited power) breeds monsters. Certainly, it is true that much of the history of the czars is a story of hideous cruelty and insensibility to

3. V. I. Semevsky, *The Peasants During the Reign of Catherine II* (St. Petersburg, 1903).

the elementary human needs and rights of workers and of much of the rest of the population.

To understand the role that the Russian worker was to play in overthrowing the czars, it is useful to take briefly into account the history of the rulers and of their acts relative to the workers' welfare.

"Of the six immediate successors of Peter I," wrote historian Sir Bernard Pares in a neat summary, "three are women, one a boy of twelve, one a babe of one, and one an idiot. Through the barrack capital of St. Petersburg . . . cut off from the life of the Russian people, brainless or squalid adventurers succeed each other."

While he was alive, Peter the Great had ordained that succession to the throne was to be by choice of the reigning czar and not necessarily in direct line of royal blood. As Peter was writing his last instructions, his strength suddenly slipped away and he could no longer hold a pen. His daughter Anna was summoned to hear from his dying lips his choice of successor. "Give all to . . . ," breathed Peter and then expired.

With the help of military officers, Peter's lusty widow, Catherine I, became empress. She was not a Russian. A servant girl from the Baltic state of Livonia, she had been the mistress of Alexander Menshikov, chief advisor to the czar, before becoming Peter's mistress and later his wife.

As the first woman to rule Russia, she was resented; and peasants whispered that their *wives* should swear loyalty to her, not *they*. She imposed ever more intolerable burdens on the serfs and spent colossal sums on her personal whims.

Catherine I reigned for only two years and died an early but natural death. She was followed by a boy of twelve. He was Peter II, grandson of Peter the Great. The lad spent all his time hunting, took no part in affairs of state, and died of smallpox at the age of fifteen, on the very day set for his wedding.

Next followed the ten-year reign (1730–1740) of Anna, a niece of Peter I. A fat woman, whose advisors, friends, and tastes were German, she was coarse and spiteful. "Evil-tempered, senseless in her love of luxury, devoured by ennui, she found distraction in the grossest cruelty and in a passion for debased forms of entertainment. She filled the court with dwarfs and misshapen creatures and her parks and gardens with every manner of beast on which she could fire from palace windows."[4] On one occasion, Anna is said to have arranged for two midgets to marry and then had them frozen to death in an ice palace for her amusement.

Besides the confiscatory taxes that she imposed, the people suffered from natural calamities during her reign. Devastating storms swept over Russia. There were famines, epidemics, and fires; and masses of people begged in the streets.

Anna's gloomy reign ended with her death from natural causes. She had named as heir an infant grandnephew of three months, who immediately became Czar and Emperor Ivan VI. It did not take long for the baby to be deposed and his regents imprisoned and for military officers to turn to Peter the Great's daughter Elizabeth. She inherited her father's love for great constructions and her mother's sensuality and peasant greed.

Elizabeth went to staggering expense to build the Winter Palace in St. Petersburg, which was to be stormed when revolution finally broke many years later. In order to make the journey between two of her palaces by boat rather than by jolting carriage, she ordered the digging of a long canal.

Extravagant beyond all reason, she owned fifteen thousand dresses at one time. Her floor is said to have been littered with unpaid bills, and her French milliner refused her further credit. During her reign (1741–1761), the conditions of serfdom were made more unbearable. There were numerous uprisings and mass flights of despairing people. It should be added in her favor that she founded the first Russian university.

During Elizabeth's reign a set of labor regulations was issued. The purpose was as much to legitimatize the excesses of the employers as to protect the employed. The regulations, promulgated in 1741, required employers, for example, to build workers'

4. Charques, *op. cit.,* pp. 121–122.

barracks near each factory, but the cost of construction was gradually to be deducted from wages. Similarly, the regulations said that employers must provide a uniform for all workers—but here again payment was to be made by deductions from wages.

In addition, 25 percent of all wages was to be withheld by management as a deposit to cover possible damages to the owners' property. Fines were imposed for infractions of factory rules, and the money thus collected was put into a fund also to be used to satisfy any claims of owners for damages.

The regulations of 1741 are instructive in shedding light on the kinds of abuses that existed and that the rules aimed at correcting. One paragraph states: "The wives and daughters of workers may only be employed in factories if they express the wish to work there, and their wages must be the same as those paid to men." The implication, of course, is that there had been enforced employment of women and that their wages had been inferior to those of men.

Peter III was Elizabeth's nephew, and he came to the throne next. Dissolute, mentally unbalanced, and incapable of governing, he was no match for his ambitious and adroit German wife, who was to become Catherine the Great. He reigned for six months. In the summer of 1762 a group of imperial guards proclaimed Catherine empress, and her husband signed a document of abdication under duress.

The most glittering period of the St. Petersburg court occurred under Catherine the Great, who had not a drop of Russian blood in her veins and no lineal right to the crown. During her reign from 1762 to 1796, Russia became one of the major military, diplomatic, and industrial powers of Europe. When Catherine came to the throne, there were 994 factories in Russia. By the time her reign came to an end, there were 3,161 factories.[5]

One of the most portentous events of her reign was an uprising led by Emelian Pugachev, an illiterate former Cossack. At first a revolt of Cossacks and ragtag elements, it grew into a serf war.

Serf workers from the mines and industrial enterprises of the

---

5. M. I. Tugan-Baranovsky, *The Russian Factory in the Past and Present* (St. Petersburg, 1898).

Ural Mountains joined peasant serfs who had fled from their masters, religious dissenters, persons of non-Russian stock from Tatar and Finnish tribes repressed by the czars, and fugitive convicts.

Pugachev's forces captured town after town along the Volga River and in the Urals. Often the gates were opened to welcome them without a fight. Landowners and their families were vengefully tortured and killed. The torch was set to their houses. Army units dispatched to quell the marauders mutinied and slaughtered their own officers. Executions by firing squad or hanging were carried out against czarist officials, merchants, and priests; village authorities were in some cases flung from church towers. In one three-month period alone, Pugachev hanged five hundred priests and officers. Among the unenforceable edicts he issued was the abolition of serfdom.

The uprising lasted for the greater part of two years, and for a time Moscow itself seemed threatened. But in August of 1774 the rebels suffered a costly defeat at the hands of czarist troops: two thousand of Pugachev's followers were lost, and eight thousand captured. At about this time, a famine caused much of the remainder of the great chaotic horde to disperse in search of food. Pursued relentlessly by mounted troops, Pugachev was surrendered by the last of his adherents. He was taken to Moscow in a cage like an animal, tried, and executed in January 1775.

The result of the revolution was more repression rather than reform.

At her death, Catherine was succeeded by her son, Paul (whether his father was Catherine's deposed czar-husband or one of her lovers is disputed). It is also debatable whether Paul suffered from occasional mental unbalance or was completely insane. In any event, his behavior was erratic at court and on the parade ground; he was fond of drilling troops, whom he had costumed in resplendent Prussian uniforms, so tight that they could scarcely breathe. He swung, like a pendulum out of control, between bestowing favors and humiliation, often upon the same person.

Emelian Pugachev, leader of the peasants' war of 1773–75. *Tass from Sovfoto*

Despite all of this, Paul was the first czar to make even a symbolic gesture toward setting some kind of limits on the amount of work that could be demanded from serfs. A manifesto urged (but did not make compulsory) that the peasant serfs be given a day off on Sundays and high church festivals, a privilege already enjoyed by Russian workers. It also recommended that the working week of a farmer serf should be divided equally between the cultivation of his master's land and of his own plot.

Often motivated by nothing more fundamental than hatred for

his mother, Paul reversed many of Catherine's policies. He also countermanded Peter the Great's rule that the reigning sovereign could choose his successor. Paul reestablished the principle of succession to the throne from father to son. He hoped in this way to eliminate palace revolutions and murders.

This did not save Paul himself from the hands of assassins. Conspirators crept into the emperor's bedroom on the night of March 23, 1801, and strangled him with a scarf. Involved in the plot were men whom Paul had exiled from the capital and then, in a change of mood, recalled; the commandant of the palace guards, in whom Paul had placed his trust; and his oldest son, Alexander I, who inherited the crown.

Alexander I was twenty-three when he came to the throne. Like Catherine the Great, he possessed ability and character. His reign began after the French Revolution, a time when the winds of liberal thought were being felt throughout Europe. In Russia even some young aristocrats were advocating emancipation of the serfs. Among these was a small group of Alexander's boyhood friends, who met regularly with him to discuss and draft reform schemes. Alexander's liberal leanings proved more sentimental than practical, but there *were* some changes for the better.

He banned the sale of serfs in the open market and set down conditions under which individual serfs might purchase a piece of land by agreement with their masters.

Any hope for extensive domestic change was submerged under preoccupations with Napoleon's march to Moscow in 1812, his inglorious retreat through the Russian snows, and the triumphant entry of Alexander's troops into Paris a year later.

Increasingly, Alexander showed signs of being haunted by guilt of patricide and the fear that he might share a similar fate. He placed his trust in no one and was suspicious of all. Napoleon called him "the northern Sphinx"; and to Alexander Pushkin, the great contemporary Russian poet, he was "the enigmatic czar."

Even his death was cloaked in mystery. In his last years he spoke often of abdicating, of enjoying the freedom of a private citizen in Switzerland or Germany. In September 1825, he suddenly went to

Taganrog on the far-off Sea of Azov to join his empress, from whom he had long been separated. It had been a childless marriage, but he had had several children by a mistress, the wife of a court official.

At Taganrog, Alexander suddenly became ill and died. The legend persisted that he had not really died, but had only vanished from sight to become a religious hermit in western Siberia, taking the new name Fedor Kuzmich. A religious recluse of that name died in Tomsk in 1864. The unlikely story gained converts in the 1920s when Alexander's coffin was opened and inexplicably found to be empty.

Alexander I was succeeded by his brother, Nicholas I, talented and tyrannical, who ruled from 1825 to 1855. The reign started with a portent of the revolution to come.

A group of young army officers, led by a brilliant staff officer named Paul Pestel, had been meeting clandestinely for almost ten years. They discussed means for infusing a measure of liberty into their country's life. At first, their hope was to bring about a constitutional monarchy with greatly limited powers for the czar.

Gradually, Pestel's views grew more extreme. Instead of a constitutional monarchy, the aim became a republic. Instead of reform, the objective expanded to revolution. Pestel's plan was for armed insurrection, the murder of the czar and the imperial family, and establishment of a temporary dictatorship to reconstruct society. In his blueprint for revolution, which he never completed writing, Pestel's papers were prophetic. Lenin's thinking, almost a century later, bore a resemblance to this predecessor's.

Known as the Decembrist conspirators because they struck on December 26, 1825, the day on which the oath of allegiance to the new czar was to be taken, they failed dismally. Some twenty-five hundred soldiers lined up in a St. Petersburg square in front of an equestrian statue of Peter the Great. They were without decisive leadership or clear immediate purpose. Nicholas ordered a loyal regiment to fire and many of the Decembrists fell. In a few hours, most of the three hundred persons directly involved in the conspiracy were rounded up, including Pestel. Later they came to be regarded as martyrs in one of the first and futile acts leading to the Bolshevik Revolution.

Czar Nicholas I personally conducted the interrogation of Decembrist suspects. The death penalty, which Elizabeth had abolished, was ordered for thirty-six Decembrists and carried out against five, generating a wave of revulsion against the czar.

There was revolution at the time in other parts of Europe and this, together with the Decembrist trauma, caused Nicholas to fabricate the most despotic regime of all. His reign marks the beginning of the Russian police state. An elaborate secret police network was established, and informers infiltrated everywhere. Any hint of intellectual dissent was suppressed. Even the slightest political offense carried a sentence of deportation to a Siberian penal settlement. Nevertheless, there were more than six hundred peasant risings, most involving limited numbers, during the reign.

Thought control was exercised through censorship. A nervous censor deleted the expression "forces of nature" from a scientific work. Another censor stopped the publication of an arithmetic book because he suspected a code might be contained in the rows of dots between the numbers of the problems. Even Pushkin was required to submit his work before publication to the czar's personal scrutiny because the poet had been a friend of many of the Decembrists.

No detail of regimentation evaded the czar's attention. He personally designed uniforms for students, bureaucrats, and other categories of the population. The bureaucracy grew large and blundering. Once ten wagonloads of documents dealing with a single case of contract fraud were sent from Moscow to St. Petersburg, and all disappeared unaccountably on the way.

Illogically, during this regime of tyranny, the Russian worker achieved a notable improvement in his status. During the thirty-year reign of Nicholas I, the realization developed among the owners and managers of Russian industry that serf labor was not necessarily to their advantage.

The shortcomings of captive workers became apparent with the replacement of primitive hand methods by simple automatic machinery. There was no motivation on the part of the serf factory worker to improve his skills and output, because there were no

incentives, no rewards. Serf labor was inefficient and undepend-
able. It could not be otherwise.

In 1837 a group of manufacturers in the Moscow area wrote to
the minister of finance to complain that serfs could not be used
where thought and judgment were required. Mere physical exertion was one thing; initiative was another. The crux of the complaint was that these ignorant workers were an increasing burden
because they and their children had to be fed, regardless of the
contribution they made to production. It was not the *principle* of
serfdom that the factory owners found objectionable; it was,
rather, that they did not wish to be saddled with the *cost* of feeding workers who did not earn their keep. The manufacturers
wanted to be released of their legal responsibility for the mainte-
nance of their serfs.

It became clear that only by the creation of a free labor force
could Russian industry be profitable and make significant technological advances. Slave labor and technological progress could
not coexist.

In 1840 the czar issued a decree authorizing factories to free
their serf workers if they wished. They were not obliged to do so.
Nor was it an outright emancipation. There were restrictive conditions. Those released were called "free workers"—and that is the
term we shall use in referring to them—but they were not free
workers in the modern sense by any stretch of the imagination.
Moreover, peasant serfs, the majority of the population, were in no
way affected by the decree.

The factory serfs whose owners chose to free them were given
passports permitting them to travel within Russia and to look for
work under conditions they negotiated with their employers. From
their earnings they paid their former lords a fixed sum, a kind of
installment payment for their release. They kept the remainder to
provide for themselves and their families. Their wages were low,
far less than those paid to foreign workers. The so-called free
worker had an incentive to improve his productive abilities and
thereby his wages. Several factories, in fact, were forced to close
because the workers, once at liberty to do so, left to find more
advantageous jobs.

Earlier in this chapter, we spoke of a category of free workers who had never been serfs. These freemen had been artisans, shop-keepers, and the like, who had voluntarily switched to employment in industry. They always had had an incentive to improve their skills because they worked for a negotiated wage, even though they were usually prevented from switching places of employment.

These originally free workers and the workers who were released from serfdom in 1840 were those most desired and sought after by industry:

> Data for most Russian industry, excluding mines and some food-processing branches, show that the proportion of free workers in the factory labor force rose from 32 percent in 1770 to 50 percent in 1812 and 87 percent in 1860. As early as 1825, almost 95 percent of all cotton textile workers and 93 percent of leatherworkers were free, as were the great majority of workers in linen and silk manufacturing. Pos-sessional peasant [serfs working in the possessional factories described earlier] and serfs of the gentry [those belonging to a landowner] formed the great bulk of the labor force in mining, in metallurgical manufacture, and in the branches of the textile industry controlled by the nobility, who used their own subject workers to process the flax, hemp, and wool their estates produced. Long before serfdom was ended by the czar's decree, much of Russian industry had learned that slavery and advanced technology were incompatible and made an unprofitable combination.[6]

There was another industrial development of special importance under Nicholas I. In 1837 he built the first railroad in Russia, a short line between St. Petersburg and an outlying palace. Five years later, tracks were laid between Moscow and St. Petersburg. It reveals something of the inflexible character of the czar that he insisted on the tracks being straight as an arrow; there is not a curve for the full four hundred miles.

The Nicholas Railroad is a classic case of czarist exploitation of the Russian worker. In the words of one historian, "All the sorrows and sufferings" of the Russian worker are focused here. "For a whole decade many thousands of peasants were forced to work at its construction with nothing but their hands and a few

6. Harry Schwartz, *Russia's Soviet Economy* (Englewood Cliffs, N.J.: Prentice Hall, 1954), pp. 61–62.

primitive tools, as they stood up to the waist in the marshes. As a rule they were not only paid low wages, but often had to wait months for their pay. Strikes were dealt with by military force and corporal punishment; the workers were only kept quiet by vodka, which was freely sold on the spot, and the sale of which was encouraged by the authorities as it brought good profit to the State in revenue."[7]

A Russian poet, N. A. Nekrasov, memorialized the workers' hardships in a poem, "The Railroad," in 1865. One stanza reads:

> The road is straight; its banks are narrow;
> Rails there are, and posts and bridges . . .
> And Russian bones line that road.
> Do you know how many there are of them, Vanya?
>> We labored in the heat and in the cold,
>> Our backs were eternally bent,
>> We lived in dugouts, we starved and froze,
>> Were soaked in rain and died of scurvy. . . .
> The foreman robbed us, officials flogged us,
>> Poverty crushed us.
> We suffered all,
> We, who are the warriors of God
> And the peace-loving children of toil.[8]

There was a considerable growth of Russian industry under Nicholas I. Cotton, metallurgy, and sugar refining developed. Protective tariffs were imposed to eliminate the competition of superior and cheaper foreign products.

Nicholas' life ended in failure. Russia's military power, which had come to be feared throughout Europe, was shown by the Crimean War to be a sham. The root cause of the war was Russia's long-standing ambition to expand into Turkey and acquire Constantinople (now Istanbul), which would have given Russia an outlet to the Mediterranean Sea. Among those opposed to Russia's designs were England and France, which dispatched fleets to the Black Sea and landed troops on the Crimean peninsula. With foreign soldiers on Russian soil and the city of Sevastopol under

7. Turin, *op. cit.*, p. 27.
8. *Ibid.*, p. 28.

siege, Nicholas died, demoralized and exhausted. He had been stricken with a severe chill and had neglected himself. At the time, it was widely believed that he had taken poison, and this suicide theory is still held by many historians.

In ending serfdom for the factory worker, the reign of Nicholas I closed an epoch in the history of the Russian working man, but exploitation and hardship continued. There were three more czars before the revolution to create a "workers' state."

3 The Free Workers and the Czars, 1855–1894

NICHOLAS I's historic act of freeing factory workers from serfdom was overshadowed by the even more far-reaching reforms of his son, Alexander II. This was unanticipated since the new czar came to the throne at the age of thirty-seven with a reputation as an ardent conservative who would protect the interests of the nobility, the landowners, and the factory proprietors. The Russian toiler had little reason to regard the latest ruler with hope. "God is too high and the emperor is too far" ran a Russian proverb, reflecting the worker's despair, bred of generations of misrule.

Before considering the changes that occurred under Alexander II, let us survey some aspects of the Russian worker's life of that era.

The rate of infant mortality in workers' homes was very great. An observer of the period wrote that "it may be confidently asserted that out of every ten children born, eight die before they reach the age of ten years, nor is the cause of this hard to find. We will suppose a child is born in the winter in a Russian cabin, gasping for breath in foul air and stench, badly nourished. . . . After this perilous stage of childhood comes the time when the children run about and catch the cholera or scarlet fever."[1]

Children went to work at an early age. There was an absence of virtually all child life in Russian villages because the youngsters were employed at the factory workbench or in the fields; their faces are said to have conveyed the same gravity as that of Russian adults. Horse-drawn vehicles for hire in every Russian town were often driven by workers' children as young as nine or ten years of age.

Little medical care was available to Russian workers. Most qualified doctors served the upper classes, who could afford to pay, and not impoverished workers. Some factories, mines, and even entire towns had no trained doctor, but were dependent on practitioners of folk medicine. Even graduates of medical schools were usually out of touch with contemporary developments and clung to outdated theories and cures. Russian physicians are said to have been typically enemies of fresh air and exercise.

In some respects, the Russian worker's diet of the period differed little from that of Russians of a century earlier or, for that matter, of today. A staple of the worker's table then, as now, was *borscht*, a soup made with beets or cabbage (sometimes with meat as well). Many Russians believed, as they do now, that, served too hot, soup imposed a burden on the heart to pump cooling blood to the stomach. Other Russian delicacies, still much in favor, were sour cream and ice cream.

In the latter part of the nineteenth century, the era we are now considering, the worker seldom tasted meat, except at Easter, after the long Lenten fast, when even the poorest tried to include meat in the holiday meal. At other times, workers usually had to be content with black bread, kasha, and, in cold weather, lard or tallow. Sugar was a luxury which the worker's family could seldom afford, even though sugar made from the beet root was comparatively cheap in Russia.

The Russian taste in beverages has not changed. The Russians have always been great tea-drinkers. The working-class Russian

1. George Carrington, *Behind the Scenes in Russia* (London: George Bell & Sons, 1874), pp. 160–161.

not uncommonly drank many glasses (never cups) of tea at a sitting. It was always exceedingly weak. According to one folk belief, strong tea caused paralysis. When a sugar cube was available, it would be dunked, a corner at a time, into the glass of tea and nibbled bit by saturated bit.

Another enduring favorite was a ciderlike, dark drink called *kvass*. It was, and is, a hot weather favorite. Made from fermented black bread, it was more powerful in its alcoholic effect than a first sip might have indicated.

Happily, warm sheepskin was cheap; and so was fuel, so that poor Russian workers did not, as a general rule, suffer greatly from the country's severe winters. A warm pelisse (a long, fur-lined coat) was priced at levels that most workers could afford. Cold air was excluded from houses by double windows, and paper was used to seal the edges of the windows during the winter.

One of the hazards of life for the Russian, particularly in winter, was fire. Most houses were built of wood and, in cities, constructed very close together. A rule, apparently not rigidly enforced, required that no fire be lighted or kept burning in a house after eight o'clock in the evening. In spite of this rule, fires were rather frequent. However, fire departments were efficient, and conflagrations were often put out quickly. Every Russian town was divided into districts, each with its own fire-watch tower.

The devoutness of the typical Russian worker has been referred to earlier. In Russian towns people were often in the habit of feeding pigeons which landed on their window sills, but they drove away other kinds of birds. This was because the dove or pigeon was the symbolic representation of the Holy Ghost. The priesthood, however, was often held in contempt by working-class Russians, because priests lived at the expense of the community. When a person was greedy or covetous, he was said to have "the eyes of a priest."

Smoking was a popular habit. Workers, who could not afford high-grade imported tobacco, smoked the raw, dried leaves of an inferior sort either in crude wooden pipes or rolled into cigarettes. Customarily, Russians inhaled deeply into their lungs and expelled the smoke through their nostrils.

The widespread poverty of Alexander II's reign was evidenced by the frequency with which beggars were seen. A British traveler wrote:

> There are great numbers of beggars in every Russian town, profes-
> sional beggars who exhibit their sores and nakedness, and who usually,
> after the fashion of beggars, spend the alms received in drink. Even
> in the daytime these seem badly off enough, being scantily clothed,
> and often hardly clothed at all. At night . . . they pay a few kopecks
> for admission to a house where standing room and shelter is provided
> for them. There they huddle together like sheep in a yard on a cold
> night. They fight for the possession of the corners, and lucky is he who
> gets one, as he can go to sleep quite luxuriously.[2]

Useful observations of the Russian worker's mode of life were provided by a Danish literary critic and historian, Georg Brandes, who visited Russia for three months in 1887. Here are some excerpts from his account:

> In the cities, the Russian common people are found in the genuine
> Russia teahouses, where they have the melodies ground out for them
> in the organs, and enjoy the pleasure of having music at tea. There
> also the workman or the peasant is generally to be seen on his Friday,
> or when he has got a little too much in his head, with his harmonica
> in his hand, that instrument which demands so little skill and has
> superseded the balalaika of earlier times. I shall never forget a slightly
> intoxicated young workman in Smolensk, who was reeling along happy
> in the middle of the street, working away on his accordion while the
> inhabitants from all the street doors accompanied his wanderings with
> looks and smiles.
>
> [The scene in a Moscow park on Sunday]: In the park, on the great
> lawns, the common people were collected in great swarms. But neither
> song nor music was to be heard, nor a single shout or noise of any
> kind. The people amused themselves in perfect silence.
>
> [A St. Petersburg workers' district]: The workmen in this district
> lived in barracks. One hundred and fifty workmen slept in a narrow
> room. Bunks were built up on the walls, so that they lay and slept as
> in berths on board a ship, except that these bunks of benches were

2. *Ibid.*, p. 60.

so wide that the workmen lay with their heads against the walls and their feet toward the middle of the floor. There was no other furniture in the room, nothing whatsoever—no pillows, no carpet, no chair, no table. The furnishings were exactly like a dog-kennel. This unfortunate condition depends on the fact that there are everywhere found contractors who keep hundreds of workmen in the vicinity of the large manufactories, to rent them out as soon as there is need of them. The food they get is a porridge which is scarcely cooked. The rest is uneatable bread and undrinkable *kvass* with a few pieces of cucumber in it.

The superstition of the people still continues. In a manufacturing region in middle Russia, where I was staying, the lightning struck several times, or some other misfortune happened, on Trinity Sunday. To avert the wrath of Heaven, this year, the workmen asked the monks in a cloister some miles away to lend them the miracle-working image of "the Blessed Virgin with three hands," which in that district is regarded as endowed with holy, supernatural power; and this picture was brought to the country town, with great pomp, in a special railway car, accompanied by the singing of priests and the swinging of censers. The people collected at the station in such numbers that those who were on the front part of the platform were compelled to take refuge in the railway carriage, to escape being crushed. The picture was brought into the church, where a Te Deum was sung. The day passed without either storm or accident, and there was not a workman who had a doubt as to the supernatural cause thereof.[3]

There was no reason to think that Alexander II would be capable of the kind of enlightened leadership needed to cope with the misery and ferment in the country. His father had gotten him involved in state business early in life, but his overriding passions were military organization and parade ground drill. His tutors tried to wean him to intellectual pursuits, but failed.

Russia's humiliation in the Crimean War, largely because of widespread official incompetence and corruption, had caused anger in every sector of the population and raised hostility to the regime.

The catastrophe to imperial Russia's vast war machine was taken everywhere as proof of the bankruptcy of the Russian political and

3. Georg Brandes, *Impressions of Russia* (New York: Thomas Y. Crowell Co., 1966; reprinted from 1889), pp. 31, 34, 37, 38–39.

social system. The rotten core of this system was peasant serfdom, which still enslaved farm workers in the predominantly agricultural country. A people in bondage could not be expected to serve national interests effectively in war or in peace.

As his first priority, Alexander II negotiated a peace with England, France, and his other enemies to end the Crimean conflict. Then, to the astonishment of all and the dismay of the landowners, he turned his attention to abolishing peasant serfdom and to other reforms.

In March 1861, the Edict of Emancipation was issued. It was a momentous event in Russian history, of comparable importance to Lincoln's Emancipation Proclamation two years later. Although it applied directly to the peasant part of the population, Alexander II's document had an important bearing on the worker sector, as we shall see.

The terms under which the peasants received their freedom differed from section to section of the vast country because of greatly varied conditions, but in all cases obligated the peasant, who was still subject to flogging for breaking the law, to long-term payments for the small piece of land he received for himself.

Peasant women searching for work in Moscow around the 1860s. *Novosti from Sovfoto*

The Edict of Emancipation had a tremendous impact on industrial development. The effect was not immediate, but was seen in the 1880s and 1890s in a big spurt in Russia's industrial growth. The edict made part of the peasantry available for employment in industry. The peasant was now relatively free to seek work in factories or other enterprises if he wished. Many did. A large, free labor force, previously lacking, gradually appeared.

One class of peasants, the so-called "household serfs," who worked in the manors of the gentry, received no land. Some were retained in the new circumstances by their former masters as paid domestic servants. But many were released and had no choice but to look for jobs as workers.

All other peasants who wished to leave the land had to receive permission from the village council. The council was held responsible by the government for payment of taxes and of the installments due on the land acquired by peasants. A peasant who wished to find work in a factory had to convince the council that his obligations would be fulfilled in his absence. Only then was a passport, necessary for travel outside the village area, granted.

Frequently, one or two members of a family would leave to find work in the towns; the rest would remain behind to farm. They would choose a town where others of the village had already settled. Often a job had been prearranged by friends or relatives in a factory, or as a blacksmith, carpenter, or gardener, for example. Many villages depended for their prosperity on money sent by these town workers. In periods of depression the factory hands, who had never cut their ties, could return to the family land. Often, when a worker grew old, he would return to his village and turn over his urban job to a son or other relative from home.

There was another way in which the emancipation helped nurture industry and enlarge the ranks of Russian workers. Members of the nobility who wished to leave their reduced estates could cash in the state bonds they had received for their lost land. Many invested this money in the development of factories, transport, or trade.

It should be noted, too, that the peasants now found themselves with money in hand from the sale of their crops, whereas their

masters had usually paid them before in potatoes and other produce. More people were now able to buy goods. A mass market for
many types of products, previously lacking, was in the process of
formation. This was a stimulus to industry.

Alexander II pushed ahead to initiate other reforms. Reasonably
representative local councils were elected in 1864 with responsibility in the long-neglected fields of education and public health.
Local county councils were established and became the incubators
for political parties.

Permission was renewed for travel abroad. The army was given a
thorough reorganization. Trial by jury was established, and some
genuinely independent magistrates were appointed. The number
of university courses was expanded, and admission requirements
were eased to let in more students from non-noble classes. Press
censorship was relaxed, and so were the restrictions on publication
of foreign books.

During this period the first translation of the writings of Karl
Marx appeared in Russia. It dealt with weighty topics, and probably the authorities saw no harm in permitting its publication since
so few people could comprehend it.

However, the authorities were wrong: key sections of Marx's
writings were simplified and distributed among Russian workers
and peasants and exerted a significant influence on later revolutionary events.

For the first time in many generations, the Russian masses felt
sentiments of gratitude toward the czar. Alexander became known
as the "Czar-Liberator" because he ended peasant serfdom and
initiated other reforms. Yet, as has often been the case in history,
the main effect of granting long-denied rights was to whet the
appetite for more rights.

A small segment of the population that was to play a decisive
role in Russia's history saw the reforms as halfway measures. The
intelligentsia, an influential group of well-educated, articulate
people, including young aristocrats, believed that real political and
social justice was possible only by drastic changes in the very

system of government. Through their pamphlets, as time went on, they reached and influenced the thinking of many workers.

Inevitably, there were implacable extremists. These were mainly students. They wanted revolution and the czar's overthrow.

Many students felt a sense of personal responsibility toward the underprivileged peasants. They felt guilt for the injustices inflicted on the serfs by preceding generations. In this respect, their sentiments were perhaps not very different from those of some American students in recent times in relation to the blacks. A plan of action followed by the Russian youth was not very different either from that adopted more than a century later by the Americans.

Russian students went to live among the peasants as teachers, nurses, blacksmiths, and shopkeepers. They brought with them literature to indoctrinate the peasants in the evils of state and class.

The young activists were not entirely successful. Most peasants were interested only in land, not in politics. The country people were suspicious of these strange city youth and in some instances tied them up and delivered them to the police. Often, puzzled by the leaflets distributed to them, the peasants would take them to the local priest for an explanation, thereby exposing the young revolutionaries' illegal activities.

On April 16, 1866, a young student named D. V. Karakozov pointed a pistol at close range at Czar Alexander II as he was getting into his carriage following a stroll in a St. Petersburg park. Karakozov had been connected with an extremist group of students, but he was regarded by his compatriots as unbalanced and was acting entirely on his own. The bullet missed, but its impact on the life of the country and on the future progress of reform was immediate and tragic.

A campaign of repression was instigated by the czar and his advisers. A main target was the entire student body. Stern controls were imposed on university life, the press, and a number of other activities.

The reaction of the young revolutionaries, although they were relatively few in number, was to intensify their efforts. Fanatic, ingenious, and dedicated, some were caught and punished; but this did not deter the others.

Their main weapon was the bomb. They made several attempts to blow up the czar's train. Each time, the explosives failed to detonate or were set off by the train that always preceded the imperial train. Once the revolutionaries bought a small building near the railway and dug a tunnel from it under the tracks, where they planned to detonate a large mine when the czar's train passed. The czar escaped because at the last minute a decision was made for the train to depart from Moscow in another direction.

The terrorists infiltrated the czar's very residence. A workman who was part of the movement had been employed in making repairs in the dining room of the Winter Palace and had smuggled in small sticks of dynamite over a period of time. On February 17, 1880, the explosives were set off, killing a large number of people; the czar was saved only because he was in another part of the palace awaiting a visiting prince, who was thirty minutes late.

Alexander II made one last attempt at pursuing his program of reform to head off revolution. He abolished the secret police section created by his father. A measure of freedom of the press was reestablished. A liberal was made minister of education. Discussions were undertaken for the reform of peasant taxation and about other moves to appease the revolutionary element. It was to no avail.

On March 13, 1881, the czar was driving along a St. Petersburg canal when a bomb was thrown at his carriage. Unhurt, Alexander got out of the carriage to comfort members of his cavalry escort who were wounded. The would-be assassin, a young man named Rysakov, was arrested.

With the shout "It is too early to thank God," a second assassin, by the name of Grinevetsky, flung another bomb between the feet of the ruler. The fire and metal ripped into Alexander's legs, stomach, and face. His last words were: "Home to the palace, to die there."

The bomb killed more than the person of Czar Alexander II. It extinguished the last hope of a constitutional solution to Russia's problems. Genuine shock and some grief were felt throughout the land except by the small band of revolutionaries. Leaders of the revolutionary organizations who escaped abroad conceded that there was no evidence of public sympathy for their deed.

The murdered czar's son was Alexander III, who was thirty-six when he inherited the throne. He was six feet four inches tall, and the stories handed down about his strength surpass those about Peter the Great. Czar Alexander III could bend a horseshoe in his bare hands or an iron poker or a silver plate.

Once at dinner, the Austrian ambassador hinted that his government might mobilize two or three army corps to settle a dispute in the Balkans. Quietly, Alexander III picked up a silver fork, twisted it into a knot, and tossed it onto the ambassador's plate. "That," he said without raising his voice, "is what I am going to do to your two or three army corps."

The czar was devoted to his family, but dominated them as he did his empire. He walked like a great bear and was gruff, outspoken, often brutally direct, and clear-thinking; he hated court pomp and felt that the true Russian virtues lay in simplicity. He wore his trousers until they were threadbare and his boots until the soles could no longer be repaired. To Queen Victoria of England he was "a sovereign whom I do not look upon as a gentleman."

Alexander had always shown deep respect for, and loyalty to, his father, although he had not agreed with his reforms. It was thought that loyalty to his father's memory might cause Alexander to promulgate a plan for the establishment of a national representative body to advise on legislation. Only a few hours before the assassin's bomb had torn life from him, Alexander II had given his approval to this measure—the first step toward possible constitutional government.

This was not to be. The new czar was fixed in his ways and determined on Russia's course. His father's assassination had convinced him, if indeed he had ever had any doubts, that his misgivings about reform were valid.

In a manifesto on his accession to the throne, Alexander declared that he would rule with "faith in the power and the right of autocracy."

Repression became the watchword of most of the thirteen-year reign of Alexander III. The terrorists responsible for Alexander II's death were rather quickly rounded up. Grinevetsky had been killed by his own bomb. Five others were executed. Those who did not escape across the border were jailed or sent to Siberia. The revolutionary organizations were, for the time being, destroyed.

The czar's policy was easily defined—to turn the clock back. This was his logic: reform had resulted in treason and regicide; the way to prevent further deterioration of authority was to return as far as possible to conditions prior to the 1861 Edict of Emancipation.

Village priests were expected to report to the police on any parishioner who expressed politically dangerous thoughts. Some priests were obliged to submit their sermons in advance to censorship by higher ecclesiastical authorities. The press was gagged by restrictions including a ban on the employment of anyone politically suspect.

There were periodic student strikes and disturbances with which the authorities dealt harshly. The universities lost all semblance of independence. By the hundreds, students were expelled from the universities, imprisoned, or sent to the army. During all of Alexander III's reign, a form of martial law was in force in one or another section of the country to suppress disorders.

Terrorist plots against the czar were repeatedly discovered. In 1886 the imperial train, a favorite target as we have seen, was derailed as Alexander and his family were in the dining car eating pudding. Twenty-one people were killed. The dining car roof fell in; and, with his enormous strength, the czar lifted it on his shoulders long enough for his wife and children to crawl out uninjured.

In the spring of 1887, five university students were arrested in St. Petersburg. They had concealed a crude and unworkable bomb inside a hollowed medical dictionary and were charged with planning to murder the czar. One of the students was named Alexander Ulyanov. He was hanged in May of that year. As he walked to the gallows, his mother was at his side, repeating over and over, "Have courage. Have courage." Ulyanov had a younger brother, aged seventeen at the time, named Vladimir. He later changed his name to Lenin and was the leader of the Bolshevik Revolution.

The vigor of Alexander III's repressive policies caused the zeal and effectiveness of assassins and revolutionaries to wane, at least temporarily. Among the masses of ignorant and tradition-minded Russians, there was veneration mixed with fear for this emperor-czar-autocrat, who was in effect a one-man government and whose only responsibility, as he and many of his subjects saw it, was to God. Yet, more and more, Alexander III felt it wise to live within the protective custody, as it were, of his own palaces.

Early in 1894, Alexander III caught influenza and began having trouble with his kidneys, which developed into nephritis. Reluctantly, he followed his doctor's instructions and went to the Livadia Palace, an imperial summer residence on a promontory overlooking the Black Sea, for a long rest. There he died on November 1, 1894 (the room was used fifty-one years later by Franklin D. Roosevelt when he attended the Yalta Conference and lived in the palace).

During Alexander III's reign enormous impetus was given to industry. Alexander saw in the expansion of Russian industrial capacity the best way to achieve a power balance with the more advanced nations of Western Europe.

Alexander was fortunate to inherit from his father the services of Sergei Witte. A burly man of great height and with a large head, this brilliant administrator had worked his way up from railway stationmaster to minister of communications, and finally to the position of minister of finance. Astute, resourceful, coarse, he wrought sweeping changes in Russia's economy over a period of a dozen years.

He was responsible for the laying of the Trans-Siberian Railroad in 1891–1905. The 4,350-mile-long track, at first a single line with sidings, made it possible to travel from Moscow to the Pacific in eight days. Before that, the journey took a year. The rail line opened an incredibly vast territory to settlement and industry.

"As Minister of Finance," recorded Witte, "I was also in charge of our commerce and industry. As such, I increased our industry threefold."[4]

4. Count Sergei Witte, *The Memoirs of Count Witte* (New York: Doubleday, 1921), p. 76.

He accomplished this by attracting large numbers of foreign industrialists and traders, tempting them with tax exemptions and government subsidies. Great sums of foreign capital were invested in Russia during this period. Many new factories were founded.

During Alexander III's reign (1881–1894), the number of factory workers almost doubled, reaching a total of nearly one and a half million. Much of the labor force was concentrated in a relatively small number of giant factories. St. Petersburg was a center for metallurgy. Textile plants were found in St. Petersburg, Moscow, and Lodz. Oil refineries were situated in Baku on the Caspian Sea. On the Black Sea were yards for construction of naval and merchant ships.

This was the period in which the industrial proletariat was formed. We shall hear the word "proletariat" often as we follow the development of the Russian worker. It means "the laboring class," "the class of wage earners"; and before the Russian Revolution, the word was used by reformers and revolutionaries to imply an *exploited* class.

During this phase of industrialization, the exploitation of labor was at its worst. The working day for men, women, and children seldom ran less than twelve to fourteen hours and even as long as sixteen or eighteen hours. It was not unusual for children to start work at the age of ten. Women ordinarily brought their children with them to the factory. Wages seldom provided more than a subsistence standard of life. Often workers were paid only twice a year, which forced them into perpetual debt.

Fines were arbitrarily imposed and deducted from wages. Housing, when it was furnished by a factory, was crowded and often unsanitary; workers were frequently crowded together in huge factory barracks, with people of all ages and both sexes sharing quarters. A faded photograph in Moscow's Museum of Secret Communist Meetings evokes the atmosphere of the period; it shows a factory dormitory, shabby, squalid, crowded—the beds are tiers of narrow shelf-like bunks attached to the walls.

A firsthand evaluation of the Russian worker of the period is obtained from the writings in 1870 of an Englishman who lived in

Russia for four years as director of an iron works. "It is curious to observe," he wrote, "that although a Russian workman is capable of imitating everything that is shown to him, his power of initiation is generally nil. . . .

"The Russians can adapt themselves to any work. The English manager of a British-owned paper-mill, which even I was astonished to find established among the Ural mountains, was recounting to me that in England it was thought necessary for a man to have served his time for a term of years to make him a good workman; but that three months made his [Russian] men capital paper-makers, just as good as Englishmen of the same class."[5]

Most Russian workers lacked education and training. The world of industry for most of them was new and strange. Often a job that was accomplished by one person in other countries required three or more workers in Russia.

The history of subjugation which we have been recounting

5. Herbert Barry, *Russia in 1870* (London: Wyman & Sons, 1871), pp. 269, 272.

One of the factory barracks, showing the squalid living conditions of the workers in czarist Russia. *Sovfoto*

could not help but leave an imprint on the mentality and behavior of the worker. An analysis has been provided by a former British ambassador who wrote of "a trait noticed by many travellers and a theme in the British colony in czarist days—the Russian's laziness, or, more exactly, his dislike of sustained effort and routine exertion. Doubtless the long winters, the habits of the nomad, and the lack of incentive bred by servile labor have all made their contribution to this attitude."

There was also, he continued, "the ingrained habit, many centuries old, of blind, automatic obedience to superior orders. In the eighteenth and early nineteenth centuries—the golden age of the czarist autocracy—foreign visitors, especially the French, brought back many stories illustrative of this. There was the sentry who was still posted in a remote corner of a park because, fifty years before, an empress had noticed a solitary wild flower there and said no one must pluck it; there was the French barber (Pahlen, I think), who was nearly flayed and stuffed because the empress had ordered to be stuffed a favorite dog which had been given the Frenchman's name, as it had been his gift."[6]

Early in Alexander III's reign, a few regulations were introduced to safeguard the welfare of factory workers, especially of minors. A law of 1882 provided that children between the ages of twelve and fifteen must not work more than eight hours and were forbidden to work at night. Employers were supposed to allow children free time for school.

With the general tightening of the screws of repression as Alexander's reign progressed, even these extremely modest safeguards were mostly annulled. A law of 1890 authorized night work for children; the only restriction was that the employer was required to obtain a license for this. Even children as young as ten could be put on temporary night work.

Working conditions varied greatly from area to area. In St. Petersburg, where there was a shortage of labor, conditions on the whole were better than in Moscow, for example, where workers were plentiful.

6. Sir David Kelly, "The Psychology of the Soviet Soldier," in B. H. Liddell Hart, ed., *The Red Army* (New York: Harcourt, Brace, 1956), p. 215.

In this connection an economic study notes:

> Occasionally, progressive employers provided better conditions, but these were not typical. The government from time to time sought to improve matters by legislation. As early as 1866 an act required employers to provide a minimal amount of free hospital and medical care. . . . Beginning in 1882 a system of periodic factory inspection was set up to enforce laws, and it achieved some important results, particularly in reducing the number of child workers. Legislatively, the czarist state was one of the pioneers in providing protection for workers. Inadequate enforcement, however, vitiated the actual benefits resulting from these laws, and after 1897 some of the most "extreme" protective legislation was nullified by repeal or amendment under pressure from employers.[7]

As mentioned above, factory inspectors were first appointed by the government in 1882. One of them was a professor, I. Yanzhul, who in 1882–1883 inspected 158 factories employing 84,606 workers. He found that the average working day was twelve hours, but in thirty-four factories a thirteen to fourteen-hour day was in effect. Some even had an eighteen-hour working day. Paybook records were seldom kept by factory owners, but fines for offenses were usually meticulously recorded. Professor Yanzhul found great ingenuity on the part of factory managers in arbitrarily defining offenses and setting fines. Here are some reasons for which fines were imposed: for singing songs during work hours; for bringing tea, sugar, or other provisions into the workshops; for washing underwear in the dormitories; for using the pump in the factory courtyard for bathing; for writing on walls; and children were fined for fighting among themselves.[8]

Professor Yanzhul's reports show that in some factories a large proportion of children were employed; in one factory, 26 percent were children, some under ten years old. Their average working day was twelve hours. Seventy-five percent of the children did not go to school at all. Factory owners paid little heed to the govern-

7. Schwartz, *Russia's Soviet Economy*, pp. 67–68.
8. I. Yanzhul, *Labor Conditions in the Moscow Province* (St. Petersburg, 1884), p. 83.

ment recommendation that schools should be established at the plants; most owners considered this an unnecessary extravagance.

As it grew in numbers, the new industrial proletariat became conscious of its potential strength. Resentment was growing among the workers, and also the determination to bring about change. The stage was being set for workers' organizations and for strikes. The proletariat was preparing to play a vital role in the destiny of Russia.

4 The 1905 Workers' Revolution, 1894–1905

IT was during the reign of Czar Nicholas II, son and successor of Alexander III, that workers—the proletariat—developed into an organized major force that contributed to the disintegration of imperial authority and to events that changed Russia and world history.

A variety of factors were responsible for the evolution of the workers' role. One factor was the very growth of the number of workers as industry expanded. In 1861, when the Edict of Emancipation was issued, the industrial population of Russia totaled about 700,000. By the time Nicholas II came to the throne in 1894, the number had grown to almost 1,700,000. (Nevertheless, Russia was still a decidedly agrarian country with 80 percent of the population classified as peasantry.) An enormous expansion of industry is demonstrated by these figures: between 1860 and 1900 the annual production of coal swelled from about a quarter of a million tons to 16 million tons; oil, from about three-tenths of a million tons to more than 10 million tons; and pig iron, from a third of a million tons to 2.7 million tons.

Nicholas II and Empress Alexandra

Another reason for the enhanced influence of workers was that they began to loosen their close ties with agricultural communities. As has been pointed out earlier, in the first stages of Russia's industrial development, workers were brought into the factories straight from the plow; and they maintained close ties with their native villages. Often when a worker reached old age and the demands of the workbench became too taxing, he would return to the village of his birth and turn over his place at the factory to a younger relative from the farm. At harvest time many factories would shut down to enable workers to help their relatives bring in the crops.

The weaning of the workers away from the soil was a slow process, and as late as 1922 a writer for the Russian publication *Economist* noted: "Up to the present our industrial working population considers its occupation in industry as of secondary impor-

tance and tries by all means not to lose its ties with the countryside." However, the process of loosening ties began during the
regime of Nicholas II. A survey shortly after the turn of the
century showed that in the Moscow Province, for example, more
than 75 percent of the workers had lost their ties with farm
communities. They no longer journeyed to the countryside during
the harvest season. In other areas the percentage was very much
lower, but the trend was unmistakable everywhere. Moreover, as
the worker ceased to identify himself with the peasant community,
he acquired a more pronounced sense of solidarity with other
industrial workers.

Still another factor contributed to the workers' new importance
in the history of the era. Workers displayed a greater militancy in
the formation of trade unions and in the use of the strike as a
weapon for seeking redress from grievances.

Intolerable conditions, particularly the length of the working
day, were the reason for most strikes. The working day in the
majority of factories was twelve hours or more; work at night and
on Sundays was commonplace. The continuing wave of walkouts
finally led the government, in 1897, to enact a law fixing the working day at eleven and one-half hours, but even this limitation was
not rigidly enforced.

An investigation into the shocking conditions of Moscow factories was conducted for the authorities by one Professor I.
Ozerov. He found "a very depressing picture of the workers' lives."
The Ozerov report continued: "Everything depends on the boss.
He must be given a bribe if one wants a job; he can dismiss all who
fail to greet him. Fines for being even five minutes late are very
heavy. But what is even more disgusting is the practice of searching the person. A worker is searched every time he leaves the
factory: sometimes he is asked at the gate to unfasten his suit or to
take off his boots, even in cold and frosty weather. 'We are
searched because we are suspected,' wrote a worker, 'but when
some of the members of the administration are suspected, or when
they have misappropriated a large sum of money, it is excused as
kleptomania.'"

"In 1899," continued Professor Ozerov's report, "the administration of a factory issued an order that the lavatory was to be used only four times a day. For additional use a fine of 10 kopecks would be imposed. This rule was approved by the factory inspector and was in force up to 1901. Then a factory inspector, Obukhovsky, refused to give his sanction to it, but the administration still kept a clerk sitting at the entrance to the lavatory to register the names of those who used it more than four times. The next morning the offenders would be fined at the rate of 10 kopecks for each additional visit to the lavatory. Workmen devised all kinds of ways of satisfying this natural need, and often it is done in the workshop, as the offender cannot afford to pay the fine."

Labor unions and strikes had always been forbidden; but from the beginning of Nicholas' rule, walkouts began to take place with increasing frequency at factories in St. Petersburg, Moscow, and other industrial centers.

Strike committees were formed in many factories. In some instances, committees in several factories in the same branch of industry coordinated a so-called "group" strike. In June 1896, for example, more than thirty thousand workers in twenty-two cotton factories in St. Petersburg walked off their jobs in unison. When the police repressed such organizational activity, secret cells were formed in factories.

Increasingly, too, strikers began to voice *political* as well as economic demands. Besides demanding improvements in factory conditions, the strikers insisted that the czar grant some form of representative government.

In 1902 a police officer named Serge Zubatov came up with a bizarre idea for diverting the alarming labor unrest into economic rather than political channels. The plan was to organize labor unions with undercover police sponsorship and protection, the aim being to secure better working conditions from the factory owners. The workers would enjoy immunity from arrest for forming illegal unions. The police, by their quiet participation and guidance, could keep an eye on the revolutionary leaders and ensure that labor activity would be directed only against factory owners and not against the czar. Zubatov thought, in fact, that his "police socialism" would win the allegiance of workers to the regime by obtaining economic gains. The employers, for their part, could not rejoice at the appearance of labor organizations, but they were persuaded that they would be better off to have the workers controlled by the police than by revolutionaries.

As part of the program, Moscow University professors held educational sessions in factories. Clubs and savings banks were organized for the workers, who were only too happy to utilize any auspices that would enable them to organize more tightly. The movement did achieve some minor improvements in conditions for textile and metallurgical workers.

The most important, and, of course, unintended, legacy of "police socialism" was that it taught great numbers of workingmen how to join together in a common effort. When the police abandoned the project, the lessons were later turned against the police and the government.

The experiment rather quickly took an unexpected turn. Some police agents developed a genuine sympathy for the workers' cause, political as well as economic. One agent organized a wave of crippling strikes in the summer of 1903 in Odessa, Baku, and other southern centers.

Repression followed. The minister of the interior was Vyacheslav Plehve, a professional policeman who had enhanced his reputation by conducting the roundup of conspirators in the plot that took the life of Alexander II. Flogging became the punishment for strikers. Political assemblies of any kind were outlawed. It was necessary to get written police permission for a social gathering of more than a few people. Students were forbidden to walk together on Moscow and St. Petersburg streets. As had been the fate of the minister of the interior who had preceded him, Plehve was blown to pieces by a bomb in July 1904.

The odd alliance of police and workers came to an end; but one of the most active and highly placed police agents, a young St. Petersburg priest, Father George Gapon, had in the meantime committed his sympathies to the workers. Early in January 1905, with the nation in the grip of strikes by increasingly resolute workers, Father Gapon set about organizing a quixotic mass march to the Winter Palace to present demands to the czar peacefully.

Some Russians still clung to the romantic notion that the czar, their "little father" in the old Russian tradition, would protect them if only he could be made aware of their miseries. Gapon drew up a petition that named as the oppressors "capitalistic exploiters, crooks and robbers of the Russian people" as well as the "despotic and irresponsible government."

The day before the march was to be held, Gapon informed the authorities of his intentions and asked that the czar be present to accept the petition. With the knowledge of the czar, the authorities brought additional troops into the city. The czar remained at a palace outside the city, where he had moved following an incident two days earlier: a cannon firing a salute at a ceremony had used a live charge and the shot had landed near the Winter Palace, wounding a policeman at his post not far from Nicholas himself. Although an investigation allegedly showed it to be an accident, the czar chose to live outside of the city for a time.

The floridly worded petition reflected the sufferings of the workers and their yearning for reform. This is an invaluable document for the insight it provides into the worker's view of his sorrowful situation:

> Your Majesty! We, the workmen and citizens of St. Petersburg, our wives, children and parents, have come to Your Majesty to beg for justice and protection. We are all paupers, we are oppressed and overburdened with work; we are often insulted for no reason, we are not regarded as human beings but are treated as slaves; we suffer and we have to bear our sufferings silently. We are driven further and further into the abyss of poverty, anarchy and ignorance; we are strangled by despotism and tyranny, so that we can breathe no longer. We have no strength at all, Your Majesty. Our patience is exhausted. We are approaching that stage when death is better than the continuance of our intolerable sufferings.
>
> And now, we have walked off our jobs and we have announced to our employers that we shall not go back to work until they satisfy us. We want only a little. We want to live, but not to suffer as though we were in prison or in exile. . . .
>
> Your Majesty! We are here, many thousands of us; we have the appearance of human beings, but in fact we have no human rights at

all, not even the right to speak, to think or to meet for discussion of our requirements or the steps to be taken for the improvement of our conditions. We are turned into slaves by your officials. . . . Every worker and peasant is at the mercy of your officials, who accept bribes, rob the Treasury and do not care at all for the peoples' interests. . . . We, the Russian workers and people, have no voice at all in the expenditure of the huge sums collected in taxes from the impoverished population. We do not even know how our money is spent. The people are deprived of any right to discuss taxes and their expenditure . . .

Specific demands in the petition included: an eight-hour working day, an improved scale of wages, a minimum wage for unskilled workers, better sanitary and medical conditions in places of work, and no reprisals for participation in strikes.

The czar on whom the petitioning workers based their hopes was a well-motivated but ineffectual man. Nicholas II was twenty-six years old when his father died. Intelligent, gentle, devoted to his family, deeply religious, and of considerable personal charm, Nicholas was also weak-willed, lacking in courage, impressionable, easily influenced by flattery, and pathetically inexperienced. Furthermore, Nicholas had acquired an aversion to reform early in life. At the age of thirteen, wearing a sailor suit, Nicholas had stood at the bed of his mutilated and dying grandfather, Alexander II, whose reward for reforms had been an assassin's bomb.

The reign of Nicholas II was punctuated by turbulent events. He was borne by irresistible forces like driftwood in rushing rapids. There were occasional pools of deceptive quiet, currents that moved briefly against the river's flow; but the ever-gathering energy defied any outcome but a final plunge over a fatal cascade. The day that the workers tried to present him with their petition helped ensure the inevitability of the final outcome.

Many facets of the worker's life are revealed through the sensitive eye of Russian short-story writer Anton Chekhov (1860–1904), who considered "absolute and honest truth" to be the aim of fiction. In *Three Years*, written in 1895, Chekhov describes the lot of workers employed by a rich Moscow merchant whose "warehouse is not a commercial establishment, but a torture chamber." The fifty workers live three or four in a crowded room in the basement of the merchant's home. At meals, several eat from a single plate. If they go out in the evening, they must be home by nine; and if the merchant detects vodka on their breath, they will be whipped. The worker grows up obsequious and eager to attain a degree of authority in the establishment so that he can exercise the same cruel discipline over future young assistants. It should be added that in *The Cherry Orchard*, Chekhov presents a different kind of merchant, decent and fair-minded.

In "Vanka" we witness the appalling plight of a nine-year-old orphan boy, who has been sent from his village to learn a trade from a shoemaker in a distant town. The boy writes a letter to his grandfather in whose village home he had been happy, pleading to be taken away:

> Last night I got a thrashing. The patron dragged me by my hair into the yard, belabored me with a shoemaker's stirrup, because, while I was rocking their brat in its cradle, I unfortunately fell asleep. And during the week, my mistress told me to clean a herring, and I began by its tail, so she took the herring and thrust its face into mine. . . . Food there is none; in the morning it's bread, at dinner kasha, and in the evening again bread, as for tea or sour-cabbage soup, the patrons themselves guzzle that. They make me sleep in the vestibule, and when their brat cries I don't sleep at all, but have to rock the cradle.

The problems of the worker in big industry was a frequent concern of Chekhov. In "A Doctor's Visit" (1898), he describes the atmosphere:

> For the young doctor called out from Moscow to a big cotton-mill in the country there is something sinister about the whole atmosphere of the place, about the workmen timidly taking off their caps to his carriage, the workers' cottages with the washing outside, the bare enclosed court-yard, like a prison, with its five factory buildings, warehouses, workers' huts, all covered with a grey film, and the uncanny metallic noises made by the watchmen as they beat the hour from each building in turn.[1]

1. Walter Horace Bruford, *Chekhov and His Russia: A Sociological Study* (New York: Oxford University Press, 1947).

"A Woman's Kingdom" (1894) is the story of a young woman who has inherited a metal works employing 1800 men. She wants to improve their conditions; but their laziness, lack of self-respect, and coarse, dishonest ways foil her good intentions. The atmosphere of an industrial plant is powerfully portrayed:

> Anna Akimovna disliked and feared those huge dark buildings, warehouses, and barracks where the workmen lived. She had only once been in the main building since her father's death. The high ceilings with iron girders; the multitude of huge, rapidly turning wheels, connecting straps and levers; the shrill hissing; the clank of steel; the rattle of the trolleys; the harsh puffing of steam; the faces—pale, crimson, or black with coal-dust; the shirts soaked with sweat; the gleam of steel, of copper, and of fire; the smell of oil and coal; and the draught, at times very hot and at times very cold—gave her an impression of hell. It seemed to her as though the wheels, the levers, and the hot hissing cylinders were trying to tear themselves away from their fastenings to crush the men, while the men, not hearing one another, ran about with anxious faces, and busied themselves about the machines, trying to stop their terrible movement. . . .
>
> And she had not once been in the workpeople's barracks. There, she was told, it was damp; there were bugs, debauchery, anarchy. It was an astonishing thing: a thousand rubles were spent annually on keeping the barracks in good order; yet, if she were to believe the anonymous letters, the condition of the workpeople was growing worse and worse each year.

Anna's visit to the rooms of a workman's family provides an intimate vignette of the setting, the people, and their interrelationships:

> There was no entry at No. 46; the door opened straight into the kitchen. As a rule the dwellings of workmen and mechanics smell of varnish, tar, hides, smoke, according to the occupation of the tenant; the dwellings of persons of noble or official class who have come to poverty may be known by a peculiar rancid, sour smell. This disgusting smell enveloped Anna Akimovna on all sides, and as yet she was only on the threshold. A man in a black coat, no doubt Tchalikov himself [the worker she had come to see], was sitting in a corner at the table with his back to the door, and with him were five little girls.

The eldest, a broad-faced thin girl with a comb in her hair that stood up like a hedgehog, was not more than three. All the six were eating. Near the stove stood a very thin little woman with a yellow face, far gone in pregnancy. She was wearing a skirt and a white blouse, and had an oven fork in her hand.

"I did not expect you to be so disobedient, Liza," the man was saying reproachfully, "Fie, fie, for shame! Do you want papa to whip you—eh?"

Seeing an unknown lady in the doorway, the thin woman started, and put down the fork.

"Vassily Nikititch!" she cried, after a pause, in a hollow voice, as though she could not believe her eyes.

The man looked round and jumped up. He was a flat-chested, bony man with narrow shoulders and sunken temples. His eyes were small and hollow with dark rings round them, he had a wide mouth, and a long nose like a bird's beak—a little bit bent to the right. His beard was parted in the middle, his moustache was shaven, and this made him look more like a fired footman than a government clerk.

"Does Mr. Tchalikov live here?" asked Anna Akimovna.

"Yes, madam," Tchalikov answered severely, but immediately recognizing Anna Akimovna, he cried: "Anna Akimovna!" and all at once he gasped and clasped his hands as though in terrible alarm. "Benefactress."

With a moan he ran to her, grunting inarticulately as though he were paralyzed—there was cabbage on his beard and he smelt of vodka—pressed his forehead to her muff, and seemed as though he were in a swoon.

"Your hand, your holy hand!" he brought out breathlessly. "It's a dream, a glorious dream! Children, awaken me!"

He turned towards the table and said in a sobbing voice, shaking his fists:

"Providence has heard us! Our saviour, our angel, has come! We are saved! Children, down on your knees! on your knees!"[2]

The published recollections of the life of a young worker in Sevastopol provide a vivid picture. The lad had come from his village of Kashoffka to work in the brush and broom factory of a

2. *The Short Stories of Anton Chekhov*, edited by Robert N. Linscott (New York: Modern Library, Random House, 1959), pp. 198–199, 200, 203–204.

family that had left the same village some years earlier. He later recalled the evening of his arrival in Sevastopol:

I was shown a splintered board floor in one of the sheds for a bedroom. Other apprentices and workmen were snoring in various corners. While Kashoffka had never been luxurious, I had had a bed to sleep on. I spent a wakeful and miserable night, for not only was I disappointed, but I could not bear to put my mother's pillow on the floor.

The next day I started work in the factory. . . . The contract I had made, which seemed so marvelous and advantageous to me at Kashoffka, may not appear so to others. I had pledged to work for four years without pay, receiving only an allowance of ten rubles yearly for clothing. The work to which a green apprentice was put could scarcely be more disagreeable or revolting, for some of the brushes were made from horsehair and the hair of various other animals. This was delivered in cartloads at our back entrance, clinging to bits of skin and flesh which, in decaying, had an odor like all possible stenches in the world stirred together. . . .

We all worked from sunrise to sunset, so when the weather was most agreeable we were confined for a longer term of hours. In winter we had more time for recreation. . . .

I was soon promoted from scraping the hides to boring holes in the brush handles. This was much cleaner work, and the prevailing smell was wood, a welcome change. . . .

The boss was out of the room most of the time, and when it was known that he was at a safe distance discussions were carried on which were not for his ears. I took no part at first, except to ask the meaning of words I did not know, but I soon caught on to the fact that each one of my fellow workmen, including the champion brushmaker, was a Socialist and eager for the revolution: at least, hopeful for its success. They spoke so earnestly about the rights of the workers, the injustices perpetrated by the government, the greed of the rich, that I was soundly impressed. . . . I was very much excited, especially when I found out that to be a Socialist was to have a price on one's head.

The bands of workers in the factories throughout Sevastopol had secret means of communications, kept in touch with one another, held underground meetings. I was told this in the beginning, but soon I had ample tangible evidence. A strange man entered the shop to buy brushes, and instead of buying several at a time he returned each day to select another. Like magic all socialistic conversation stopped. My companions had recognized a member of the secret police. We all might be hanged or whipped to death.[3]

It was redress from appalling conditions like those described by workers, Russian authors, and foreign visitors that the petitioners sought on that fateful Sunday morning, January 22, 1905. Columns of workers, linking arms and singing religious hymns and the imperial anthem, "God Save the Czar," began streaming out of workers' neighborhoods toward the center of the city. Flags, banners, icons, and crosses were carried. The marchers headed for the Winter Palace, where they assumed the czar to be. They also innocently thought he would receive their petition and promise to set things right. Certainly, there were provocateurs and troublemakers in the ranks of the gullible. None of the marchers reached the Winter Palace.

Cossacks and infantry had taken up positions at intersections and on bridges blocking the way. When the processions continued to move forward, the soldiers opened fire at many points in the city. According to the official count, there were ninety-two dead and several hundred wounded—women and children fell among the men. Probably, the actual count was several times higher.

Leaders were seized by the police, but Father Gapon escaped. Nicholas wrote in his diary that night: "A painful day. Serious disorders took place in Petersburg when the workers tried to come to the Winter Palace. The troops have been forced to fire in several parts of the city and there are many killed and wounded. Lord, how painful and sad this is."

From his place of hiding, Father Gapon issued an open letter to the czar denouncing him as the "soul-murderer of the Russian empire." The language was revolutionary: "The innocent blood of workers, their wives and children lies forever between you and the Russian people. . . . May all the blood which must be spilled fall

3. Harry E. Burroughs, *Tale of a Vanished Land: Memories of a Childhood in Old Russia* (New York: Houghton Mifflin, 1930), pp. 262–263, 264, 266, 267.

upon you, you hangman." The priest called for "an armed uprising against czarism."

Not only was Gapon being sought by the police for organizing the march, but leaders of the Social Revolutionary Party, one of the underground political groupings which were developing in Russia, issued their own death sentence on him. They suspected that Gapon had provoked the march as a secret police-agitator. They reasoned that he knew the soldiers would open fire and had counted on this to teach the workers not to try future protests.

In April 1906, Father Gapon was discovered in an abandoned house in Finland. Apparently tracked down by vengeful revolutionaries, he had been hanged.

The authorities made the mistake of expelling from St. Petersburg a large number of the participants in the fatal protest. Those expelled carried firsthand accounts of the atrocity to all parts of the empire, arousing passions everywhere. The day became known as "Bloody Sunday," and it lit the fuse to ten months of disturbances and terror and a breakdown in authority. This Revolution of 1905, as it was called, brought Czar Nicholas II to partial capitulation.

Nineteen hundred and five was a year of disasters for the czar in foreign affairs as well as at home. Russia had been expanding into Asia (ambitions of empire in that direction had entranced Nicholas ever since his travels as heir to the throne). The Russians annexed Port Arthur in China, and Nicholas entered in his diary: "At last we shall have an ice-free port." Russia occupied Manchuria and penetrated northern Korea.

Japan tried to negotiate a division of the region into spheres of influence. However, the czar's government was inflexible in the belief that if war resulted, Japan would be defeated; and Russian victory would head off the growing threat of revolution within Russia. On February 8, 1904, Japan, without a declaration of war, attacked Port Arthur and bottled up part of the Russian fleet. The outbreak of hostilities did, in fact, produce a brief spontaneous outpouring of patriotic support for the czar.

To the astonishment of the world, tiny Japan inflicted a series of

Cossacks and czarist infantry at the Winter Palace open fire on the procession of workers led by Father Gapon on January 22, 1905. This was the "Bloody Sunday" that began the Revolution of 1905. *Soviet Life from Sovfoto*

defeats on the Russians on land and sea. Port Arthur fell to Japan in January 1905. The reaction of a group of workers at a Volga River town was described by a Belgian technician employed at the factory:

> When I arrived back at the works after the lunch hour I found the square in front of it filled with prostrate bodies. Employees—all more or less hopelessly drunk. Inside there were only a few foremen about and none of them were sober. In the lathe shed there were Grisha and two other mechanics. They weren't drunk, but they were discussing in low tones an item in the newspaper. Port Arthur had surrendered to the Japanese. Grisha noticed me as I came in and said that it didn't look as if there would be any work done that afternoon. I could see that for myself, but I asked why. Were all our men desirous of drowning their grief in vodka?
>
> "Oh no, sir," answered Grisha, "the workers don't look upon the fall of Port Arthur as a calamity. They're celebrating."
>
> "Don't they know that it's Russia, not Japan, that's lost Port Arthur and, very likely, the war?"
>
> "Why, sir, it matters very little to them who has Port Arthur. But they just feel a mortal blow has been struck to czarism and so they just have to celebrate."[4]

Under the peace terms signed in September 1905 at Portsmouth, New Hampshire (President Theodore Roosevelt had been instrumental in bringing the two sides together), Nicholas lost Port Arthur, northern Korea, most of Manchuria, and all of the allegiance he had temporarily attracted from the people in the initial flush of patriotism. The "small victorious war," as it turned out, sharpened the contempt of the workers and other dissidents for the regime. The humiliating, demoralizing news of repeated Russian disasters in the course of the war was a primary cause of the Revolution of 1905.

Workers participated to the fullest in the events of 1905 and played a decisive role. Throughout the year there was a rash of street demonstrations and strikes. That year witnessed the greatest

4. Boris Silver, *The Russian Workers' Own Story* (London: George Allen & Unwin, 1938), p. 13.

strike movement in Russia's entire history. During the course of the year, at one time or another, practically every worker was involved. The chief economic demand was for an eight-hour working day. Political demands came to the forefront as the ordinary workingman joined with the radical intelligentsia in calling for the abolition of one-man rule and the convening of an assembly to draw up a constitution for a democratic republic.

Defiance of authority mounted. One morning, the czar's uncle, Grand Duke Sergei, governor-general of Moscow, was assassinated as he was driving through a Kremlin gate. Again, the instrument of death was a bomb. Police officials in scattered parts of the country were killed. Almost invariably, the assailants escaped.

The reckless spirit spread to military units and there were mutinies; in the Black Sea, sailors aboard the battleship *Potemkin*, enraged when they were served bad meat, threw their officers overboard and steamed away from the escort fleet. The dreadnought proceeded along the coast, indiscriminately bombarding towns until lack of fuel forced the crew to sail into a Romanian port, where the ship was interned.

From the Vistula River to the Ural Mountains, the peasants were less interested in obtaining a parliament than in acquiring more land. "All the land for the peasants" became their battle cry, and they methodically took possession of property belonging to the landowners.

In despair, Nicholas made this diary entry: "It makes me sick to read the news, strikes in schools and factories, murdered policemen, Cossacks, riots. But the ministers instead of acting with quick decision, only assemble in council like a lot of frightened hens and cackle about providing united ministerial action."

Meetings were being held unceasingly in factories, universities, among professional people, and in the budding political parties to discuss grievances and formulate plans of action. Everywhere the demands were for freedom of speech and assembly, new laws to humanize working conditions, a better deal for the peasants, and, above all, a freely elected national legislature and a constitution. A constitution would set forth the peoples' rights and fix limitations on the powers of the czar and his ministers. Until this time, as we have seen, the czar's powers were without limit, and the peoples' rights were only those he might care to bestow for any period of time.

Events built to a climax in mid-October 1905. A general strike brought life in St. Petersburg to a standstill. Workers left their jobs, closing down many factories in other parts of the country as well. Railroads came to a halt from one end of Russia to the other. Schools closed. Newspapers ceased publishing. Food was becoming scarce as distribution became erratic. Electric power was turned off. Throughout the day, streets in the capital were crowded with people listening to speakers. Red flags of revolution flew everywhere. In the countryside the peasants turned to violence and began stealing cattle and setting manor houses on fire.

There was an absence of effective authority, and in these chaotic conditions a new workers' organization appeared in St. Petersburg and seized the helm. It sprang into being on October 26 from the ashes of the union framework Father Gapon had created in the factories.

The new organization was called a *soviet* (the word means "council") of workers' deputies. It was composed of representatives elected by strike committees in each factory. The example of the St. Petersburg soviet was followed in other cities where soviets were also formed. The principal organizers were members of the diverse socialist parties.

Within a few days, a leader of the St. Petersburg soviet emerged in Leon Trotsky, a rousing orator and member of the Social Democratic party. Trotsky, largely self-taught, a Jew from southern Russia, was twenty-six at the time. Arrested in 1898 for revolutionary activities, he was exiled to Siberia, escaped in 1902, and continued his work from France, Belgium, and Germany. In London he collaborated with Lenin in publishing the revolutionary newspaper, *Iskra* ("Spark"), which was smuggled into Russia.

Under Trotsky's magnetic leadership, the St. Petersburg soviet immediately assumed the status of a rival authority to that of the czar's government. It adopted the tactic of concentrating on the demand for an elected assembly to draw up a constitution.

Trotsky and his associates threatened to wreck any factory that did not shut down. Units of soldiers marched into the city to reinforce the garrison. Military guards were stationed in front of every public building. The danger of street battles with the workers mounted.

The crisis in the capital lasted four days. Almost all normal life came to a standstill. The forces controlled by the soviet and those loyal to the czar confronted each other. Then Czar Nicholas acted.

On October 30, 1905, Nicholas issued a manifesto promising to grant most of the yearned-for reforms. A legislature would be elected by the people. Almost all new laws would require the approval of this Duma. Drawn up by Witte, the manifesto promised "freedom of conscience, speech, assembly, and association" to Russia's people.

The document, however, also reasserted the principle of autocracy and gave the czar exclusive power to appoint and dismiss government ministers. He also kept for himself complete control over defense and foreign affairs and the very important right to issue laws independently in an emergency, which *he* could declare at any time.

It fell far short of establishing a constitutional monarchy, but it did close the era of absolutism, in which unlimited power was vested in the person of the czar. The principle of representative government was granted, and it could not afterward be completely revoked.

Count Sergei Witte (he had received his title from the czar in gratitude for his role in concluding the war with Japan) was appointed president of the Council of Ministers, equivalent to prime minister. It was his job to make the new system work.

Most of the political groups regarded the outcome as a clear-cut victory. Not so, though, did revolutionary elements of the Social Democrats, who controlled the St. Petersburg soviet. They were not appeased and wanted the overthrow of the czarist regime, not concessions. Their attitude was expressed by Trotsky, writing in the just-established newspaper, *Izvestia* ("News"): "The proletariat knows what it does not want. It wants neither the police thug Trepov [the main police official] nor the liberal financial shark Witte: neither the wolf's snout, nor the fox's tail. It rejects the police whip wrapped in the parchment of the constitution."

The soviet began to issue weapons secretly to its supporters. It

Barricades in the workers' quarters of St. Petersburg, 1905. *Sovofoto*

called for another general strike, but many workers did not respond this time and stayed at their jobs. An attempted third general strike met with even less enthusiasm. Nevertheless, scattered strikes and disturbances and especially assassinations by terrorists continued in many parts of the country.

The showdown came in December 1905. The government moved against the St. Petersburg soviet and arrested 190 men, the bulk of its members. Trotsky was banished to Siberia, escaped to Vienna, and eventually reached New York.

In Moscow the soviet was led by Lenin, who ordered the erection of barricades in workers' quarters and proclaimed a provisional government to replace the czar's. It was a desperate venture by several thousand men. The insurrection lasted a week. A number of revolutionary workers tried to capture a railroad station to disrupt rail traffic and prevent the arrival of troop reinforcements. They were repelled. Finally, additional troops arrived, fired artillery against the barricaded rebel strongholds, and crushed the rebellion. More than a thousand lives were sacrificed. The Museum of the Revolution and other museums in Moscow contain detailed diagrams that show the disposition of forces during the fighting. In one tabletop scale model, small figures of czarist cavalry are shown charging the barricades as workers fire from them. The largest barricade in the city was eighteen feet high. Like the more than one thousand others in Moscow at the time, it was constructed of barrels, wood, stone, and whatever junk the revolutionaries could assemble.

Paintings in Soviet galleries romantically depict Lenin atop flaming barricades, red flag in hand, heroically leading the workers. Many years later, Lenin called the events of 1905 a "general rehearsal" for the Revolution of 1917.

5 The Fall of the Czar, 1906–1917

IN the Museum of the Revolution in Moscow, paintings depict the struggle between the working and ruling classes. All are propagandistic in their sledgehammer presentation of the working-man's case. Many are unintended caricatures of heroes and villains. Yet they are useful in providing a sense of the era and of the workers' condition.

One painting is called *Paying Off*, and the lengthy caption is typically melodramatic:

> The artist shows a group of workers who had come to their employer for a settlement. Separated from them by sturdy banisters, he—their lord and master—relaxes in an easy chair. His fat face expresses self-satisfaction, his pose confidence; it seems that no power on earth can dislodge his filthy, corpulent body. However, suffice it to glance at the faces of the workers to see how insecure is the position of the capitalist. The people confronting him are not ignorant, humble slaves, but enlightened workers insisting on their legitimate rights. The eyes of the workers burn with hatred. They seem ready at any moment to tear down the banister and wreak vengeance on their hated enemy.

The deep-rooted animosities suggested by the painting and its caption help explain why the czar's manifesto of October 1905 did not have an immediate effect in quelling the strikes and other disturbances.

The continuing walkouts, riots, and mutinies perplexed Witte who, in drawing up the manifesto, had assured the czar that it would bring peace and order to the country. On the one hand, Witte tried making more concessions while authorizing punitive measures on the other.

Czar Nicholas II was having second thoughts about the wisdom of his manifesto. The difficulty in pacifying the country caused him to lose confidence in Witte. On January 25, 1906, the czar wrote to his mother: "As for Witte, since the happenings in Moscow [the uprising of the soviet led by Lenin] he has radically changed his views; now he wants to hang and shoot everybody. I have never seen such a chameleon of a man."

This was a harsh judgment of a genuine statesman, who had given such faithful service; but in May of that year the czar asked for Witte's resignation.

Witte took the dismissal with characteristic bravado, declaring to a member of the court: "You see before you the happiest of mortals. The czar could not have shown me greater mercy than by dismissing me from this prison where I have been languishing. I am going abroad at once to take a cure. I do not want to hear about anything and shall merely imagine what is happening over here. All Russia is one vast madhouse." (He later returned to spend the last nine years of his life in Russia in relative obscurity.)

In Witte's place, after a brief interlude, the czar appointed Peter Stolypin, who had been minister of the interior. A burly man, Stolypin had his roots in rural nobility. Only forty-two years old when he became prime minister, this bearded, energetic, eloquent man had first come to public attention by his conduct in the 1905 peasant uprisings. On more than one occasion, as governor of a province, rather than order troops to bombard an insurgent village, he had walked in unarmed to persuade the rebel leaders to desist from violence.

Stolypin labored on two fronts. First of all, he worked relentlessly to establish law and order and to stamp out terrorist activity. So-called field courts-martial were established, which dealt quickly with terrorist attacks on local officials and police. Sentence and execution were carried out within a few days after a suspected assassin was caught.

During the summer of 1906 about six hundred men were executed on gallows, and the hangman's noose became known as "Stolypin's necktie."

The toll of victims of terrorist bullets and bombs was even greater: some sixteen hundred officials, soldiers, and police were assassinated. There were a number of attempts on Stolypin's life as well.

On the second front, Stolypin grappled with the fundamental causes of Russia's troubles. More land was transferred to peasants. He created a whole new class of small peasant landowners (by 1914, nine million Russian peasant families owned their own farms), who suddenly had a stake in stability. Viewing this from exile, the revolutionary leaders despaired lest the peasants should entirely lose their motive for revolution.

The condition of the workers was perceptibly improved, too, but less dramatically. Wage levels rose in some industries. A beginning was made in providing genuine health and accident insurance for workers. By 1914 over two million workers were enrolled in sick benefit funds. The most important strides were made in education in the industrial centers. From 1908 onward the number of primary schools rose rapidly, and it is estimated that in 1914 half the children of school age were attending classes.

In 1906 labor unions were finally legalized in individual factories, but not on a nationwide basis. Within a little more than a year, total union membership had risen to 250,000. In the latter part of 1907, most unions were wiped out in one of the recurrent waves of government repression.

The czarist regimes helped prepare the way for revolution by their unwillingness to tolerate moderate and reasonable trade unions until too late. It has been observed in this connection:

The history of czarist policy toward labor organization is a tragic story of wasted opportunities. In the early spontaneous strikes of the seventies and eighties, the demands of the workers were moderate. Ordinarily, they struck against reduction of wages, and occasionally they demanded freedom to elect a "headman" to negotiate with the employers on behalf of the workers. The answer of the authorities was to crush these incipient organizations by arresting the leaders and more active workers and condemning them to prison or exile. Labor organizations were consequently forced into conspiratorial channels, and the hostility of the government helped to divert the grievances of the workers from economic to political programs.[1]

If the government had encouraged labor unions on the Western European and American models, Russia's story might have been a different one. If such unions could have achieved improvements in wages, hours, and working conditions early in the process of industrialization, the Russian worker would have acquired a stake in the community and in its preservation. This was not to be, and in Professor Fainsod's words: "The grievances which might have found an outlet and a remedy in collective bargaining became the fertile soil for extremist appeals. State policy barricaded the road to reform and opened the flood gates to revolutionary upheaval."[2]

It will be recalled that one of the main concessions granted by Czar Nicholas II's manifesto in October 1905 was the election of a legislature whose approval would be necessary for the issuance of almost all new laws.

Voting for this first Duma took place in March 1906. The right to vote was bestowed rather widely. This had been one of Witte's last acts, and it may have been the one that exhausted the czar's patience with him. Ballots could be cast by nearly all factory workers. Political parties, now legal and active, ranged from conservatives dedicated to the czar, on the right, to the revolutionary Social Democrats on the left. The nonrevolutionary, liberal groupings, which were in the forefront in demanding reforms, scored a great victory.

The 524 members, among them workers, met on May 10, 1906, and immediately made brash demands upon the czar—the release

1. Merle Fainsod, *How Russia Is Ruled* (Cambridge, Mass.: Harvard University Press, 1953), p. 28.
2. *Ibid.*, p. 30.

of all political prisoners and the replacement of the czar's government ministers by those named by the Duma. When these were rejected, the Duma members unanimously voted censure (a resolution by a legislative body expressing disapproval), which under normal parliamentary law would force the government to resign. The Duma had no weapon to compel this. Speaker after speaker delivered denunciations of the czar's government.

It was not long before the czar acted. On July 21, 1906, the Duma was dissolved—only two months after it had first convened. The simple posting of a government announcement ended its life. That night about two hundred members of the legislature made their way to the nearby city of Viborg in Finland and issued an appeal to the Russian population to resort to passive resistance, to pay no taxes, and to send no recruits to the army. No one in Russia paid any attention to the appeal.

Elections were arranged for a new Duma, but even more liberals, again including a number of workers, were elected, and the invective hurled at the government was even more intense. One deputy, using vituperative and sometimes profane language, accused the czarist army of training its soldiers for the sole purpose of repression of the working class; he urged the troops to join the people and overthrow the government. Taking these seditious words as his cue, Nicholas proclaimed the dissolution of the second Duma, which had proved as troublesome to him as the first, on the grounds that it was plotting against the czar. Thirty Social Democratic members—representatives of the workers—were exiled to Siberia. The second Duma was disbanded on June 16, 1907, three months after it had assembled.

Now Stolypin took steps to guarantee that the next crop of deputies elected to the parliament would be more acceptable. He changed the election rules even though laws issued by the czar had prohibited any such alterations without the Duma's assent. Now the right to vote was limited to fewer people and concentrated in the hands of the nobility and landowners. Whole sections of the country were excluded from voting.

The result was that the third Duma, which assembled in March 1908, was composed mainly of conservatives, palatable to Nicholas; and after serving its full term of five years, it was reelected with practically the same personnel.

Its members included forty-five Orthodox priests, among the most reactionary elements in the land. The socialistic Labor group, which had ninety members in the first Duma and 201 (the largest block of any party) in the second, was reduced to thirteen in the rigged third.

This conservative Duma was able to work harmoniously with the czar's government, and as time passed, it even began to rally the confidence and support of a broad public by taking an increasingly independent and constructive stand on some issues.

A relative calm began to settle over Russia, and worker unrest was less frequent. The strong, competent hand of Peter Stolypin was mainly responsible.

It was common in imperial Russia for the police to infiltrate agents into underground revolutionary groups and for informers to provide the police with information, as much to ensure the informer's immunity from arrest as for money. One such shady character was named Mordka Bogrov, a revolutionary and a police agent; no one knows where his ultimate loyalties lay. This double agent was allowed to continue his illegal activities while providing the police with regular reports on the underground.

On September 14, 1911, Czar Nicholas and government officials attended an opera performance in the city of Kiev. Bogrov was given a ticket by the police so that he could help guard Stolypin by spotting any dangerous revolutionaries who might be in the audience.

During the second intermission as Stolypin rose from his seat in the first row of the orchestra and turned his back to the stage, Bogrov leveled a revolver at Stolypin's chest and fired two shots at close range. Summarizing the episode, the czar included a singular understatement in his diary: "Poor Stolypin had a bad night."

Stolypin lingered for five days. Bogrov was hanged, and four police officials were suspended for negligence. It was never completely clear for whom Bogrov was acting. It may have been a revolutionary act, but the suspicion has persisted that Bogrov pulled the trigger on behalf of highly placed reactionaries who despised Stolypin for the liberal concessions he had made to the Duma, to the peasants, and to the workers during his years (1906–1911) in office.

The economic circumstances of the Russian worker changed little in the period covered by this chapter, and what changes did occur were mostly to his disadvantage. A study by a Professor A. Manuilov, published in 1912 in Moscow, showed that during the years 1901–1909 workers' wages increased by 18 percent; but prices of food, clothing, and other commodities increased by more than 37 percent on the average. The prices of some essentials exceeded the average considerably: rye bread, for example, went up by 57 percent, and rye flour by 72 percent.

Professor Manuilov wrote: "Owing to the rise in the cost of living and in house rents, the average annual earnings of the Russian worker in 1910 ought to have been at least between 232 and 237 rubles to cover food alone: and house rents had also gone up considerably." Yet the average workers' wage in the Moscow Province was only 243 rubles a year at that time and 186 rubles in nearby Vladimir Province. The annual average for workers throughout the entire country was 244 rubles.

World War I began in 1914, and Russia's participation on the side of the Allied Powers against Germany and Austria-Hungary lasted until 1917. There was a surge of patriotic fervor at the outset. Czar Nicholas came out on the balcony of the Winter Palace, and a large crowd greeted him with an enthusiasm that would not have been predicted. The capital's German name of St. Petersburg was changed to the more Russian Petrograd.

After initial military successes, the Russian army began to suffer defeats in the face of superior artillery. At the end of only ten months of war, Russian losses stood at 3,800,000 soldiers killed, wounded, and captured. Gaps in the ranks were hurriedly filled by untrained men of all ages, often without guns. Vast territory of the empire was surrendered, including all of Poland, which had been a Russian possession. A munitions shortage became a national scandal. Russia's allies supplied arms, and there were brief flurries of victory; however, the irresistible course was downhill to disaster.

The dead alone in the Russian army numbered possibly 2,500,000 by the time fighting ended in 1917.

We have already seen how catastrophic reverses provoked radical changes in Russia following the Crimean War and the Russo-Japanese War. The same was true for World War I.

Disillusion set in among the people at the incapacity of their rulers to provide adequate support for the massive army in the field. No worker's family was without a relative in the army. Rage, frustration, hatred, and despair filled the hearts of the people. Invasion by foreign countries has always unified the Russian people, but they saw their patriotism sapped by a government they held in contempt; by a German-born czarina, the Empress Alexandra, whom they suspected of treason; and by Rasputin (a self-styled religious mystic who acquired extraordinary influence over the royal family), whom they regarded as a tool of, if not a spy for, the Germans.

It was in these circumstances that the Russian worker again assumed a role of central importance in the unfolding drama during the final months of 1916. Russia's economy, which had experienced steady growth before the war, began to show symptoms of sagging under the strain.

In the years before World War I, the country's productive might increased, especially in mining, steel production and other metallurgy, and textiles. Although the rate of growth was impressive, Russia was far behind Western Europe and the United States in industrial development. In coal production, for example, Russia's output in 1913 amounted to 36,000,000 tons, compared with 517,100,000 in the United States and 190,100,000 in Germany. The gap in pig iron production was equally dramatic. The Russians produced 4,600,000 tons whereas the United States was turning out 31,500,000 tons and Germany, 16,800,000.

Almost all machine tools, lathes, grinders, and the like in Russian factories were imported; the machine-building industries were in the most rudimentary stage. Similarly, the country lagged in the production of electric power and chemicals. There were no factories at all in Russia manufacturing cars or trucks.

No fewer than thirteen million men had been moblized into the army, and about half of them were serving at the fronts. Most had come from the farms. Less food was reaching the factory worker and other inhabitants of the cities, partially because the war fronts had first priority, but also because the farmers were holding back grain against emergencies. Food shortages were felt in the urban centers in the autumn of 1916. Lines grew longer day by day at food stores in Petrograd.

A number of factories were forced to shut down for lack of coal and raw materials. The German blockade had cut off normal imports of cheap coal from Wales through the Baltic Sea. Rail shipments of coal, iron, and copper from Russia's mines were handicapped by a shortage of trains; the railway system, hard-hit by the war, was staggering under the burden of supplying both units at the front and the home economy.

Russia began the war with 539,549 freight and passenger wagons; and by the end of 1916, losses and breakdowns had reduced these to 174,346. The number of locomotives had been drastically reduced from 20,071 to 9,021. A further toll was taken by the severe winter of 1916–1917, when one spell of extreme cold caused the boilers of 1,200 of the remaining locomotives to freeze and crack open.

The first sign that home-front discipline was crumbling presented itself in October 1916, when strikes, reflecting discontent in general, and food shortages in particular, began spreading from factory to factory. Two infantry regiments were called out in Petrograd to help the police clear the streets of striking workers; but instead of obeying orders to disperse the workers, the soldiers opened fire on the police. Cossack units galloped to the scene and charged the soldiers with drawn swords, herding them back into their barracks. One hundred and fifty soldiers were executed by firing squads for this mutiny.

It must be kept in mind that the troops in the capital at this time were not crack units. The best-trained soldiers and those of proven loyalty to the czar either had been killed in battle or were presently serving at the front. Those on duty in the cities were mainly raw recruits whose hearts responded more to the sentiments of the striking workers than to the czarist banners under which they marched.

The storm was gathering. It struck with blinding suddenness out of the black clouds of discontent and anger of a hungry people. Within a week it had left political devastation in its wake.

This uprising was not the result of a plot by revolutionaries in beards and upturned coat collars, nor by organized, embittered workers. It was the human equivalent of spontaneous combustion.

On March 8, 1917, the inexplicable psychology that motivates crowds suddenly caused the people who were waiting in the ever-growing bread lines to abandon patience. Women bundled in dark clothes, shawls, and boots against the bitter cold and intermittent snow broke into the bakeries and took all they could carry. The main street of Petrograd began filling with protesters, mostly women, demanding bread. A procession of striking workers threaded its way from the stilled factories into the city's center. Cossack cavalry was called out, but there was no violence.

The next day, March 9, found even larger crowds in the streets. Bread shops again were broken into. Again the Cossacks appeared, but their attitude toward the crowd was not hostile. There were reports, though, of police firing over the heads of columns of workers.

On Saturday, March 10, the protests swelled. Everyone seemed to be in the streets. Almost all workers had left their jobs. Schools were shut. There was no public transportation. Red banners appeared among the marchers who were calling for an end to the war, denouncing the czarina, expressing hostility to the government. There were several clashes with police, notably near the town hall; but it was increasingly evident that many of the soldiers sided with the demonstrators.

The czar was at military headquarters, more than five hundred miles from the capital, when told of the riots. He took them to be of no greater seriousness than the thousands of other street disorders that had plagued his reign. He even attached little importance to a telegram from his own cabinet ministers begging him to return to Petrograd to help them solve the urgent problem of food shortages. Almost all of his cabinet ministers offered to resign, urging Nicholas to replace them with ministers who would be acceptable to the Duma. The Duma was the only institution that still enjoyed a measure of the people's respect and allegiance. The ministers appointed by the czar were held in contempt by most of the Duma members, and there was little cooperation among them. At this point, the ministers themselves realized that the only way to salvage the deteriorating situation would be for Nicholas to name cabinet ministers who would enjoy the respect of the Duma and, in turn, the respect of the workers and other elements of the population.

Completely misjudging the temper of the times, Nicholas reacted imperiously rather than with sensitivity; he telegraphed the military governor of Petrograd: "I order that the disorders in the capital, intolerable during these difficult times of war with Germany and Austria, be ended tomorrow."

The military governor had notices posted on walls and fences as quickly as possible. They warned that all public meetings were banned and would be dispersed by force. All workers who were not back at the jobs the following Monday would be drafted immediately into the army and sent to the front.

The warnings were ignored.

On Sunday, March 11, huge crowds with flags milled in the streets and assembled at various points to listen to speakers. As the posters had warned, soldiers and police were deployed to break up the meetings. The first shooting occurred in the late afternoon on the Nevsky Prospect, the main street, and about fifty people were killed or wounded by police bullets. Before that day was over, two hundred people had lost their lives and several thousand were injured; most of these were workers and members of their families. One company of soldiers disobeyed an order to fire into the crowd and instead emptied rifles into the air. Another company shot down its commander when he insisted that they open fire into the mass of demonstrators; a company of a regiment loyal to the czar hastened to the scene, disarmed the mutineers, and marched them into their barracks.

The czar's government was in full alarm. Again a telegram was dispatched to Nicholas, informing him that there was anarchy in the capital and shooting in the streets. He scorned the message as a case of hysterics, but sent four of the best regiments from the war front moving toward the capital to quell the troublemakers.

On Monday, March 12, the day on which the posters had

ordered workers to be back at their jobs or face immediate military draft, events moved swiftly and irresistibly. The key was the military.

In the early morning hours, after a night of heated discussion among soldiers of the Volinsky Regiment, a sergeant shot a captain who had slapped him when the unit had refused to fire on the crowd the previous day. The other officers ran away to save their lives. Soon the entire regiment marched out of the barracks with a band playing at the head of their column to join the people in the streets.

It was infectious. In quick order, other famous regiments, including one founded by Peter the Great, mutinied and went over to the side of the revolution. During the day almost seventy thousand soldiers took the drastic step. Tied to many gun barrels and bayonets were red flags, the traditional color of socialism and revolutionary workers' movements.

The crowd steadily swelled in numbers. There was still no leadership, no plan, no direction. It was revolution, nevertheless, elemental and uncontrollable. The mob stormed the gates of the arsenal, where weapons and ammunition for the capital's troops were stored; and guns were distributed to workers, clerks, bus drivers, and the idle. The law-courts building was set aflame. Soon the Ministry of the Interior, the building of the military government, police stations, and other government headquarters were burning. Prisoners were set free from all of the city's jails.

The czar's cabinet ministers held meetings in a state of despair. A telephone call was made to Nicholas with the urgent suggestion that he accept the cabinet's joint resignation and appoint a government that could command the nation's confidence. The czar replied through an aide that he would leave soon for the capital, many hours away by train, and would make his decision when he arrived. Nicholas remained blind to reality until it was too late. During the late hours of Monday night a telegram arrived from the czarina that included the news that "street fighting continues, many units gone over to the enemy." Finally, Nicholas ordered his special train assembled, and early Tuesday morning he started on the long trip back.

Powerless, ignored by the monarch who had appointed them to

The storming of the Winter
Palace, Petrograd, March 1917.
Tass from Sovfoto

office, the members of the cabinet voted to adjourn. As it turned out, they were never to meet again. Before the day was over, most of them had surrendered to the Duma to be placed under protective arrest as a way of saving their lives from the mob.

Not long after midday, waves of workers and soldiers, flushed and exultant, surged through the corridors of the Tauride Palace, where the Duma met, shouting their support and asking for instructions.

Alexander Kerensky, thirty-six years old, who headed the socialist labor group in the Duma, realized that if that parliamentary body did not fill the power vacuum, more extreme elements would. He rallied the deputies to grasp the opportunity. The announcement was made that the Duma would defy the czar and accept the responsibility of acting as the government. The government would be provisional (that is, temporary) until elections could be held.

It was at this point that factory workers and soldiers began choosing representatives to form a soviet. The elections were hasty and disorganized. It will be remembered that the workers' soviet, or council, was the unit of authority that took form during the short-lived Revolution of 1905. It was quite natural in the frantic rush of events in March 1917 that the familiar body should be revived. The Soviet of Soldiers' and Workers' Deputies was composed of one delegate from each company of rebel soldiers and one delegate for each 1,000 workers. It moved into the Tauride Palace, built in the eighteenth century by Catherine the Great for one of her lovers. The Duma was meeting in a separate wing.

The sharing of a single roof was a matter of agreement and convenience to both. Kerensky later explained how it came about: The question arose "as to how and by whom the soldiers and workmen were to be led; for until then their movement was completely unorganized, uncoordinated, and anarchical. 'A soviet?' The memory of 1905 prompted this cry. . . . The need of some kind of center for the mass movement was realized by everyone. The Duma itself needed some representatives of the rebel populace; without them, it would have been impossible to reestablish order in the capital. For this reason the soviet was formed very quickly. . . . About three or four o'clock in the afternoon, the organizers applied to me for suitable premises . . . and the thing was arranged."[3]

Kerensky, the son of a provincial education official, had won a wide reputation as a lawyer for his defense of political prisoners against prosecution by the state. Already a member of the Duma, he was also elected to the newly formed soviet and rather quickly became the dominant figure in the provisional government formed by the Duma and the soviet.

If there was any question at the outset as to where the real strength lay, it soon disappeared: the workers in the soviet emerged as the central power in this period. Kerensky had to be responsive to them.

On Tuesday, March 13, the provisional government decided that the only way to prevent Nicholas II from being overthrown by violence was for him to abdicate. Only by his stepping aside voluntarily could the imperial system of government continue with a new czar on the throne. In this way, the revolutionary passions could be controlled, and order reestablished. It was decided by representatives of the Duma and the soviet that Nicholas must abdicate in favor of his son, Alexis, aged twelve and a half; the czar's younger brother, Grand Duke Michael, would act as regent (to rule in the boy's behalf until he reached maturity).

The leaders of the new government communicated with the top generals and admirals, and to a man they agreed that abdication was the only solution if they were not to lose control over their restive men.

On the morning of Thursday, March 15, Nicholas' train had reached Pskov, about 150 miles from Petrograd. It had been forced to detour because rebel soldiers controlled the rail lines around the capital. Aboard his private train he was handed the provisional government's decision to assume powers that had belonged to the czar and the generals' telegrams concurring in it. "Nicholas was overwhelmed," wrote Robert K. Massie, reconstructing the historic moment. "His face became white, he turned away from Ruzsky [the army commander in the area who had laid the telegrams before Nicholas] and walked to the window. Absentmindedly, he lifted the shade and peeped out. Inside, the car was absolutely still. No one spoke, and most of those present could hardly breathe."[4]

The choice before Nicholas was to yield or to face civil war, the collapse of the armies at the front, and the loss of his beloved Russia to Germany. It did not take him long to make the decision to abdicate in favor of his son. That night when two representatives of the provisional government arrived at Pskov for the signing of the official document of abdication, Nicholas had reconsidered —not about abdicating, but about handing the power to his son, in view of the child's incurable hemophilia. Nicholas chose to abdicate in favor of the Grand Duke Michael, thirty-nine, and the papers were signed.

So ended the reign of Nicholas II. And within a matter of hours, the monarchy itself was finished. Michael never actually took the throne. When the two delegates returned from Pskov with the act of abdication, a large crowd at the Petrograd railway station greeted the news of Michael's accession by sweeping toward the pair with murderous intentions. They barely managed to escape in a waiting car.

The revolutionary fervor in Petrograd had swiftly turned against the institution of the monarchy itself. The crowd's cry was for a republic. The workers and soldiers in the Petrograd soviet had taken an immovable position against substituting one czar for another. In the provisional government, Kerensky took the lead in endorsing the soviet's point of view. He said that if Michael took the throne, the new czar would be the first victim of a fresh outpouring of revolutionary passion. Confronted with this situation, Michael offered no resistance and quietly signed a document of abdication.

A week later, Nicholas was permitted to rejoin his wife and children at the Tsarskoe Selo Palace, about fifteen miles outside of Petrograd. The family spent five months there in an imprisonment that was at least physically comfortable. In August they were

4. Robert K. Massie, *Nicholas and Alexandra* (New York: Atheneum, 1967), p. 393.

moved to a relatively simple house in Tobolsk, Siberia. A year later, on July 16, 1918, shortly after having been moved to the city of Ekaterinburg, Nicholas and Alexandra and their children were brutally shot in a basement by secret police of the Bolshevik government, which had replaced that of Kerensky. The bodies were then dismembered, burned on a bonfire, and thrown into an empty mine shaft.

6 Marx, Lenin, and the Bolshevik Revolution of 1917

ONE of the most unusual sights anywhere in the world is the mausoleum of muted red stone trimmed with black that stands in Red Square in Moscow. What makes it unusual is the body preserved inside under glass. Not since the era of Egyptian mummies has there been so macabre an attempt to preserve a person after death.

The man in the Moscow mausoleum is Vladimir Ilyich Ulyanov, known to the world as Lenin, the leader of the revolution that, in his words, aimed to make Russia a "workers' state." He died in 1924.

Every day, long lines of people, pilgrims from all over the country, as well as many visitors from abroad, move silently and slowly across the expanse of Red Square to this shrine. A soldier with burnished bayonet affixed to his rifle stands at rigid attention on each side of the entrance. The visitor descends about three dozen steps and, turning right past another soldier at the foot of the stairs, finds himself in a lofty, darkened, stone chamber with spotlights focusing slightly pink shafts of light on a glass casket at the center. Soldiers mount honor guard at either end of it.

Lenin's face is waxen, an unnatural putty grey. The hands are visible too. The rest is covered by a stiff black material.

There has never been an official explanation of why the workers' hero has been so extravagantly exposed to public view. As one observer noted:

Nobody knows who took the original decision to keep Lenin, in the first instance, publicly displayed. One explanation, perhaps fanciful, is that Russian history is full of impostors . . . and the authorities wanted to be in a position at any time to demonstrate that Lenin was really dead. Another is that the mausoleum is the "official shrine of a new religion," in the hierarchy of which Lenin is a demigod, and it is only fitting that he should be visible to all, even as were Christian saints in early days. A simpler explanation is that Lenin was a revered figure, and Russians, who have an inordinate love for the spectacular, want to keep him around. . . . Lenin may be holy . . . but this doesn't keep people from making jokes about the mausoleum. . . . A familiar anecdote describes two peasants who emerge: one says to the other, "Just like us—dead but not yet buried."[1]

The method of embalming that has preserved Lenin's body for so long a time is a closely kept secret; some say that the secret died long ago with the embalmer.

Lenin was an historic figure of towering importance, not only to the Russian worker and the Russian nation, but also in his influence on the entire world. Victor Chernov, a fellow revolutionary and minister of agriculture under Kerensky in 1917, gave this insight into Lenin's character:

His whole life was passed in schisms and factional fights within the party. From this resulted his incomparable perfection as a gladiator, as a professional fighter, in training every day of his life and constantly devising new tricks to trip up or knock out his adversary. It was this lifelong training that gave him his amazing cool-headedness, his presence of mind in any conceivable situation, his unflinching hope "to get out of it" somehow or other. By nature a man of single purpose and possessed of a powerful instinct of self-preservation, he . . . was much like that favorite Russian toy, the *Van'ka-Vstan'ka* boy, who has

1. John Gunther, *Inside Russia Today* (New York: Harper, 1957), pp. 32–33.

a piece of lead in his rounded bottom and bobs up again as fast as you knock him down. After every failure, no matter how shameful or humiliating, Lenin would instantly bob up and begin again from the beginning. His will was like a good steel spring which recoils the more powerfully the harder it is pressed.[2]

Vladimir Ilyich Ulyanov was born in Simbirsk, now called Ulyanovsk, a small city on the Volga River, in 1870. He was named after Saint Vladimir, the first Christian duke of Kiev, capital of medieval Russia. When he became converted from paganism to Christianity, the tenth-century saint sought to impose his new religion by force on his people, not all of whom were willing to accept it. An ironic analogy can be seen in Vladimir Ulyanov's fervor after he was converted to Marxism.

This man, who became the leader of Russia's working class, did not come from that stratum of society himself. Lenin's father belonged to the minor nobility as a member of the czarist bureaucracy; he was inspector of schools in Simbirsk, a post of some local consequence; and in a period of a dozen years he increased the number of schools in the province from twenty to 434. When Czar Alexander II was assassinated in 1881, Lenin's father, a practicing Orthodox, went to the Simbirsk cathedral to pray.

Lenin's mother was of German stock, a devout Lutheran, the daughter of a doctor, who owned a large estate with serfs.

The family lived very comfortably, and Vladimir knew none of the hardships of the Russian worker of that era. Yet later he was to devote his entire adult life to the interests of the working class as he saw them. "Did he love these working people?" Victor Chernov posed the question and answered it: "Apparently he did, although his love of the real, living workman was undoubtedly less intense than his hatred of the workman's oppressor."

In 1886, when Vladimir was sixteen, his father died. The next year a formative event in his life, to which we have already referred in Chapter 3, was the execution of his brother, Alexander, for student terrorist activities. This took place during Vladimir's last year in the Simbirsk high school. It did not affect his school

2. Victor Chernov, *"Lenin: A Portrait,"* Foreign Affairs, March 15, 1924.

work: he had always received the highest marks, and he graduated at the top of his class.

Through an odd play of fate, the principal of the school was Fedor Kerensky. He was the father of Alexander Kerensky, who had been born in Simbirsk ten years before Vladimir. The elder Kerensky had been a friend and admirer of the elder Ulyanov. Their two sons were to become mortal rivals.

The sentiment of old family associations played no role in Lenin's thinking. "Nothing to him was worse," wrote Chernov, "than sentimentality. Such things were to him trifles, hypocrisy, 'parson's talk.'"

Risking embarrassment to himself because of the scandal of Alexander's execution, Fedor Kerensky wrote an enviable evaluation of Vladimir for the official records when he graduated from school:

> Very gifted, always neat and assiduous, Ulyanov was first in all his subjects, and upon completing his studies received a gold medal as the most deserving pupil with regard to his ability, progress, and behavior. Neither in the school, nor outside, has a single instance been observed when he has given cause for dissatisfaction by word or by deed to the school authorities and teachers.[3]

When Vladimir entered the university, his protest activities began. He was expelled from the University of Kazan for participation in an unimportant student demonstration. He began to study law at home and in a single year managed to complete a four-year course. When he was reinstated at the university and permitted to take his exams, he again finished first in his class. Yet his career as a lawyer was not brilliant; in his early cases on behalf of workmen and peasants accused of minor offenses, all of his clients were found guilty.

It was in this period that Vladimir discovered the writings of Karl Marx. An omnivorous reader, he applied all of his cold intelligence to mastering Marx's theories. Marx had written that the city worker would be the nucleus of world revolution; and, obsessed with the idea, Vladimir left home in 1893 to move to the big

3. Kerensky, *The Crucifixion of Liberty*, p. 10.

city St. Petersburg. Arrangements had been made for him to work in a lawyer's office, but his main interest was a Marxist study group consisting of other members of the intelligentsia, who met evenings to debate and study revolution.

Vladimir made his first trip abroad in 1895, visiting Geneva, Zurich, Berlin, and Paris. He met with Russian revolutionaries in exile and returned to St. Petersburg with the false bottom of his trunk stuffed with revolutionary pamphlets. He immersed himself in organizing workers, planning strikes, and printing antigovernment leaflets.

In 1895 he was caught in these activities, spent a year in jail in the capital, and then was sent to Siberia for three years. The main purpose of Siberian exile at that time was to remove dissidents from the cities to remote, scarcely populated areas, where they could do no harm. Those convicted of serious crimes were assigned to penal colonies; but lesser offenders, including not only Vladimir but also many thousands of workers suspected of revolutionary activities, were permitted to live a fairly normal life in the town to which they were assigned. They had to report regularly to the police, but could find jobs and live as comfortably as their means and the accommodations of the area allowed.

Vladimir was sent to the Siberian village of Shushenskoe, near the Mongolian border. His family provided him with ample money, and he was the richest man in the village. He arrived with a trunk filled with more than one hundred books and set up a household. Soon he was joined by the girl he was later to marry, a schoolteacher named Nadezhda Krupskaya, who arrived with her mother. Nadezhda had been arrested for organizing a strike and had managed to convince the police to send her to the same village by pretending she was engaged to Vladimir.

Vladimir spent a happy and fruitful three years hunting, fishing, ice-skating, reading, working on a lengthy book, *The Development of Capitalism in Russia;* and dreaming of the revolution of the working man. During his exile he and Nadezhda married. His term in Siberia ended before hers, and not long afterward he got permission to leave Russia (Nadezhda followed Vladimir later).

The year was 1900, and Vladimir's purpose in going abroad was similar to that of many other revolutionaries of the period. He felt he could do more to further the cause of revolution outside the repressive atmosphere of his homeland. In the years that followed, he acquired a wide reputation among Russians-in-exile and among underground revolutionaries within Russia. In Switzerland he helped to found and edit the previously mentioned revolutionary newspaper *Iskra.*

His articles were signed "N. Lenin," one of the several false names he had assumed. It was customary in Russia for people in illegal activities to take pseudonyms to screen their identity from the authorities. The "N." meant nothing at all. Some books errone-ously state that it stood for Nikolai. No one is sure why he chose the name "Lenin." It may have been pure invention, or perhaps it was suggested by the Lena River, not far from his place of Siberian exile.

The displaced Russians had formed a loose political organiza-tion, which they called the Social Democratic Labor party. Lenin drafted a plan of action for the party and wrote a revolutionary pamphlet titled "What Is To Be Done?," which attracted to him a large following among the revolutionaries.

In July 1903, the Social Democratic Labor party held a unity conference in Brussels with forty-three delegates present. They met in a rat-infested warehouse draped in red. The Belgian police swooped down on the meeting and gave the Russians twenty-four hours to get out of the country. They continued their discussions on the boat as they crossed the English Channel.

In London, instead of producing unity, the conference resulted in a split. The issue was how the party should be organized. One group wanted it to be open to all who wished to join. Lenin led the struggle for keeping the party small, a dedicated, professional, disciplined, fighting elite.

Lenin won by a small margin. The word "majority" in Russian is *bolshinstvo,* and those who sided with Lenin took the name "Bol-sheviks," or men of the majority. The others were "Menshiviks," men of the minority. In the opinion of the historian Charques, they were "both rather ridiculous names for movements which have made so much history." Much later, in 1912, the Bolsheviks abandoned the split Social Democratic Labor party and struck out on their own as a separate party; later still, they changed the name to the Communist party.

When the Revolution of 1905 erupted in Russia, Lenin and his colleagues were caught by surprise. They were so busy arguing among themselves that they had lost touch with developments. As was mentioned in Chapter 4, Lenin hurried back to Moscow and led the unsuccessful uprising of the Moscow workers' soviet at the barricades. He remained for a short time after the defeat, frequently changing hiding places to evade the police. One ingenious place of concealment is preserved as a museum: in a room of the Electrical Engineering Institute, a blackboard rises on pulleys to reveal a cubbyhole where, it is said, Lenin audaciously hid out. The building at that time housed the Ministry of the Interior, headquarters of the secret police. A plaque in what is now lecture room 10 reads: "V. I. Lenin (Ulyanov) used this room as a hiding place in 1905." However fictitious this legend may be, it is known that Lenin soon slipped out of Russia again.

Reforms, as we have seen in Chapter 5 followed the Revolution of 1905—the Duma gave Russia a form of representative government for the only time in its history, conditions improved for the workers, and the peasants got more land. All of these developments disheartened Lenin and the other exiles, who saw revolution slipping from their grasp. If the people could achieve their aspirations by peaceful means, there would be no reason for them to rally under the banner of revolution.

Then came World War I, and the morale of Lenin and his colleagues soared. They saw the conflict as the prelude to workers' revolution, as Marx, their teacher and idol, had prophesied.

At this point we digress briefly from Lenin's career to consider the story of Karl Marx and his tremendous impact on Lenin and on the destiny of the Russian worker. It has been said that Marx's writings exerted an influence on the modern world comparable only to that of the Bible, the Koran, and Newton's thesis on gravity.

Marx, a German, was, above all, an economic thinker and theorist. His idea that economic matters constituted the chief influence on the history of nations was original and of incalculable importance. He developed the theory of modern socialism, the system under which all factories and other means of production are owned by the government or by the workers.

The central point of the *Communist Manifesto,* written by Marx in collaboration with Friedrich Engels, is that all history is a story of class struggle—the struggle between the oppressing class and the oppressed class. In each society, the oppressed class eventually rises up, overthrows the oppressor, and then sets itself up as the ruling class. Ultimately, said Marx and Engels, a classless society will emerge from the repeated struggles.

According to this theory, in modern society the bourgeoisie (the property-owning capitalist class) is the oppressing class. The proletariat (the working class, or the "wage slaves") is the oppressed class.

The *Communist Manifesto* regarded the overthrow of the bourgeoisie by the proletariat as unavoidable: "What the bourgeoisie . . . produces above all, are its own grave diggers. Its fall and the victory of the proletariat are equally inevitable."

The clash between these two classes, said the *Manifesto,* would occur first—and this is important because what actually *did* happen was quite the opposite—in the most highly industrialized country. The revolution would then spread to countries all over the world.

Marx and Engels believed that the proletarian revolution would happen first in Germany, an intensively industrialized country, not in Russia, which was still basically an agricultural country and where the proletariat was numerically of lesser importance.

The theory continued: after the workers became the ruling class and had taken over all factories and other enterprises, they would gradually become the *only* class. No longer would there be oppressor and oppressed. It would be a society without poverty.

Another thing would happen as a result, said Marx. The state would then slowly wither away. There would, in the ultimate stage of a classless society, be no need for a state with all of its bureaucracy and police, because, according to Marx, the only reason for a state is to protect the oppressing class from the oppressed class. In a society where the only class is the proletariat, there would be no reason to have a state to protect it.

Marx also made this point: after the workers' revolution, it would be necessary to have a temporary dictatorship of the proletariat—ironhanded, nondemocratic rule by workers' leaders to prevent control from slipping back into the hands of the bourgeoisie.

Marx and Engels saw all this as an inevitable, irreversible process. They believed that they had, for the first time, uncovered laws of historical development as immutable as the law that causes the earth to revolve around the sun. They believed that with these economic-political laws it was possible to predict the future development of society. This conviction caused them to call their conclusions "scientific socialism."

Nevertheless, Marxists (followers of his views) were expected to speed up the natural process in several ways: they were to bring about the union of the workers of all countries (hence the slogan "Workers of the World Unite"), support as a matter of expediency whatever political party happened to favor "the momentary interests of the working class," and resort to violent revolution to speed the inevitable fall of the ruling bourgeois class.

Another theory developed by Marx and Engels said that wars were inevitable among the bourgeois, or capitalist, countries. Such wars would provide opportunities for world revolution by the workers because conflict would weaken the capitalists.

Lenin and his Bolsheviks based their hopes for revolution on that prophecy of war.

The onset of World War I in 1914 seemed the fulfillment of a prophecy and of a dream to Lenin and his followers. In pamphlets and papers from his homes in exile, Lenin urged the working class to oppose the war by waging civil war in each country against the capitalists. The plea fell on deaf ears. As the war dragged on without sign of workers' revolt, Lenin's spirits sagged.

The crucial winter of 1917 found Lenin and his compatriots without any definite plans in hand for revolution. There was no point in having plans as revolution seemed too remote. On January 22, 1917, only seven weeks before the Russian Revolution, Lenin spoke to a group of Swiss workers and confessed that "we older men may not live to see the decisive battles of the approaching revolution," although he thought "popular uprisings must flare up in Europe within a few years."

Lenin, living in the house of a shoemaker in Zurich, had several mundane worries on the very eve of the revolution. These were described by author Robert Payne. Lenin bought large quantities of assorted hair oils, which he dutifully rubbed into his bare scalp, but nothing he tried would stimulate the growth of any hair. During this period his mother-in-law was dying. Lenin's wife, retiring for a few hours of sleep after constant bedside vigil, asked him to awaken her if the sick woman needed anything. The next morning she awoke and found her mother dead. Completely preoccupied with his own thoughts, Lenin was sitting at a table writing. His wife chastised him for failing to call her, and Lenin is said to have replied: "You told me to wake you if your mother needed you. She died. She didn't need you."[4] Lenin had frequently been at odds with his mother-in-law from the time she had accompanied her daughter to his Siberian place of detention.

When the unexpected revolution broke, Lenin, who had been away for ten years, could think of nothing else but getting back to Russia. From neutral Switzerland it would be necessary to cross countries that were waging war on Russia or seas patrolled by German U-boats. To travel all the way around the world and across Siberia would take too long. He considered all kinds of wild ideas. His wife recalled that "From the moment the news of the revolution came, Ilyich did not sleep and at night all sorts of incredible plans were made. We could travel by airplane. But such things could be thought of only in the semidelirium of the night."[5]

The solution came from the Germans themselves. The Berlin government saw advantages in helping Lenin return. The fall of Czar Nicholas II had not taken Russia out of the war. Kerensky

4. Robert Payne, *The Life and Death of Lenin* (New York: Simon & Schuster, 1964).

5. *Ibid.*

and his associates in the provisional government intended to honor Russia's commitments and to go on fighting. Lenin had been preaching peace; and if he could actually cause Russia to withdraw from the war, it would obviously benefit Germany. Even short of that, Lenin's presence in Russia could be counted on to cause trouble for the new regime.

The German minister in Berne made arrangements for Lenin, his wife, and seventeen other Bolshevik revolutionary exiles to travel from Zurich across Germany and the Baltic Sea, to Sweden, Finland, and then to Petrograd. A special carriage was provided for the group; it was locked and guarded so they could not get out along the way and cause trouble anywhere other than at their intended destination.

Winston Churchill appraised the event: "The German leaders turned upon Russia the most grisly of all weapons. They transported Lenin in a sealed wagon like a plague bacillus from Switzerland into Russia."[6]

Lenin arrived in Petrograd on the night of April 16, 1917. He was forty-seven years old and, although he had worn a beard on and off during the years, was beardless at the time. His coming stirred excitement among Bolsheviks and other socialists. An enormous crowd welcomed him at the railroad station, and he spoke to them from the top of an armored car (the sturdy, old-fashioned vehicle with its vulnerable rubber tires is now on display on a stone pedestal in the courtyard of the Lenin Museum in Leningrad; Russian words painted on it read "Enemy of Capitalism"; the clock in the Lenin Museum tower is permanently stopped at eleven minutes to seven, the hour when Lenin died on January 21, 1924).

When Lenin arrived, more than a month had elapsed from the day the czar had been overthrown and a provisional government formed with the cooperation of the Duma and of the workers' and soldiers' soviet. The members of the soviet, including most of the Bolsheviks, who composed a minority group, believed it was necessary to cooperate with Kerensky and the provisional government. They did not want the provisional government to fall and cause a

6. Winston S. Churchill, *The Aftermath* (London: Macmillan, 1941), p. 73.

vacuum into which the monarchy might return. Furthermore, the Bolsheviks and other socialists believed in the Marxist theory that the overthrow of an autocratic form of government would be followed by a period of transition. Only later would the revolution of the proletariat occur to overthrow the bourgeois regime.

Lenin startled his listeners as soon as he arrived. In a quick series of speeches he opposed any form of cooperation with the provisional government. He was in favor of the immediate over-throw of Kerensky and his colleagues and wanted a revolution by the working class right away.

And that was not all. Lenin urged a prompt end to Russia's participation in the war. He called on Russian soldiers at the front to lay down their guns and to mingle as brothers with the enemy soldiers. They were all sons of the common people, he contended, and they should no longer slaughter each other on behalf of the capitalists.

Lenin called on Marxists in all the belligerent countries to trans-form the war into civil wars against their own governments; revolution in any one country, he contested, would light the spark to revolution elsewhere.

Not even Lenin's fellow Bolsheviks were prepared to accept these views at that time. When he addressed a meeting of the soviet a day or so after his arrival in Petrograd, he was so loudly booed that he had to leave the room.

But perseverance was Lenin's strongest card. He also had great personal magnetism, an ability to argue endlessly, to convince, to persuade. In the weeks that followed, he tirelessly reasoned with individual members of the soviet and gradually won converts. Among those he brought around was Leon Trotsky, who had led the St. Petersburg soviet in the 1905 uprising. Trotsky had re-turned to Russia from exile in New York a month after Lenin. The two men worked closely together. Trotsky was the guiding hand at first, but Lenin took over gradually.

Lenin hit on popular slogans to summarize the Bolshevik pro-gram. "All Power to the Soviet" was the main cry. It meant that all authority should be taken from the provisional government and put into the hands of the workers' councils. "All Land to the

Peasants" and "Peace, Land, Freedom" were others. "Peace" was an appeal addressed primarily to the army. "Land" was the signal to the peasants that the Bolsheviks favored the seizure of estates by the nearest peasants; nothing could endear the Bolsheviks to the peasants faster than this. "Freedom" was a promise that struck a responsive chord very widely in the freedom-starved country.

Charques aptly described it as "a breathtaking program" and examined its impact:

> Peace and bread; among all other party slogans this alone made sense to the masses. Bolshevik agitation was tireless, impassioned, brilliantly organized. At the front and in the rear, in the capital and in all the industrial and provincial centers, the propaganda of peace and the proletariat conquest of power gathered momentum. In Petrograd and elsewhere, factories were seized and "workers' control" established. In the countryside the seizure of the private estates was begun in earnest. It was now that desertion and fraternization at the front spread widely and the last vestiges of military discipline began to disappear.[7]

Yet the Bolsheviks were still in a minority among the workers and soldiers. In the middle of June 1917, delegates were elected from the soviets, which had been formed in every city and town to attend a congress in Petrograd. The assembly consisted of 285 members of the Socialist Revolutionary party, 248 Mensheviks of the Social Democratic Labor party, and only 105 Bolsheviks.

On July 1, 1917. Kerensky went to military headquarters briefly to launch personally a big offensive of the Russian army. To his credit, the troops on this occasion were quite well equipped, and the supply lines flowed with relative efficiency.

Kerensky ordered the offensive under tremendous pressure. The pressure came from Britain, France, and the United States (which had entered the war three months earlier). The provisional government desperately needed loans, and Russia's allies would grant these only if Russia held up its end of the fighting. The allies were understandably terrified that if Russia withdrew from the war, it would release many German divisions against their troops on the western front.

7. Charques, *A Short History of Russia*, p. 243.

At first, the Russians advanced on a wide front, but German reserves were brought up, and the offensive was halted. In the soldiers' committees, which had been formed after the overthrow of the czar to share authority with the officers, arguments raged about the wisdom of continued fighting. Lenin's preachings had taken root. The only thought in the mind of the peasant soldier was to hurry home to get his share of the land. There was no resistance when the enemy counterattacked, and the Russians fell back in a rout in many areas.

The news of the Russian debacle at the front reached Petrograd, where the Bolsheviks were gaining converts by the hour. On July 16 a spontaneous uprising occurred, not unlike that of the previous March. A great outpouring of humanity filled the streets, carrying red banners and chanting Lenin's demand of "All Power to the Soviets" to replace Kerensky's provisional government. Many of the demonstrators carried guns and made a disorganized attempt to seize control of the capital.

The rising was premature. Lenin and the other Bolshevik leaders were not ready to play this trump as yet. The soviet itself was opposed to the uprising. Kerensky moved quickly. He retained the loyalty of the Petrograd garrison by distributing a document that claimed to prove that Lenin was a German agent: Lenin's purpose, it said, was to undermine the home front while the Germans were pursuing Russia's armies. Regiments loyal to Kerensky seized various Bolshevik headquarters, and the arrest of Lenin and Trotsky was ordered. Trotsky turned himself in to the police voluntarily. Lenin managed to escape into Finland on a locomotive by disguising himself as a fireman. In Lenin's words, "the July uprising" turned out to be "something considerably more than a demonstration but less than a revolution."

The next big development took place two months later, at the beginning of September 1917. General L. G. Kornilov, commander in chief of the army, decided that it was his duty as a military leader and patriot to restore law and order in the army and in civilian society.

General Kornilov saw a threat to the army itself in the rising popularity of the Bolsheviks, whose party membership had swelled to two hundred thousand from fifty thousand, in the preceding March. After all, Lenin had called for the abolition of the existing bureaucracy, police, and army, and Kornilov feared the Bolsheviks would try to implement this if they came to power. The Bolshevik membership was only a handful of the total population, but the dangers were real enough. Kornilov feared that Kerensky was incapable of withstanding the mounting Bolshevik strength. He decided to eliminate the Bolsheviks and to replace Kerensky's government with a military dictatorship.

On September 8, troops from the northern front began moving toward Petrograd under orders to overthrow the Kerensky government and disperse the workers' soviet. It had the makings of a rightist, military coup d'état.

Kerensky did not know where to turn. He did not feel that he could call with confidence on the soldiers in Petrograd to defend the provisional government; they might obey their commander in chief, Kornilov, instead.

Kerensky turned to the soviet for help. The Bolsheviks at this point had achieved a majority in the soviet, and they responded with enthusiasm. Factory workers were mobilized, and Kerensky distributed weapons to them. They were called "Red Guard" battalions and were ready to do battle with the advancing army. As part of his deal with the soviet, Kerensky agreed to release Trotsky and other Bolshevik leaders from jail.

Kerensky had made a poor bargain and paid dearly. As it turned out, General Kornilov's movement quickly broke down. His troops had no stomach for a fight and immediately began to fraternize with the units sent by Kerensky and the soviet to oppose them. One of the generals who had joined General Kornilov in the attempt to seize power committed suicide.

Kerensky asked the Red Guards to return the guns and ammunition that had been issued to them. They refused.

On October 23, Lenin managed to cross the border and return to Petrograd. On the same day, the Bolshevik Central Committee, the executive group of the party, voted ten to two that it was time to stage the workers' revolution; the resolution on which they voted stated that "insurrection is inevitable and the time is fully ripe."

Feverishly, plans were laid. Orders and organizers went out to the soviets in other parts of the country. The Bolshevik intentions were an open secret, but Kerensky was powerless to forestall them.

On November 6, 1917, the Bolshevik Revolution began. The technique of the modern coup had its premiere here. Military confrontation was avoided. Instead, the effort was concentrated on seizing control of the key points to power. Armed Red Guards quickly occupied the telephone exchanges, government offices, police stations, railway stations, bridges, post offices—all the places used for communications and for control of the populace.

Bolshevik units carried out the same efficient action in other cities and towns and practically everywhere won power instantly. An exception was Moscow, where there was an intense struggle and fighting continued for a week.

In Petrograd, cabinet ministers of the provisional government who escaped immediate arrest sought refuge in the czar's Winter Palace. They were protected by a contingent of cadets and a battalion of women soldiers.

Kerensky himself slipped away in a car and headed for the front to enlist help from military commanders. He failed to rally any army units. Eventually he reached Moscow and, with the help of false papers issued by British diplomats, managed to leave Russia. He spent the rest of his life in London; Paris; Palo Alto, California; and New York, writing books and teaching university students.

On the evening of November 7, the Russian navy cruiser *Aurora,* whose crew had hoisted a red flag to signal its support of the Bolsheviks,- fired one blank shell at the Winter Palace. The alarmed women's battalion walked out of the palace carrying the white flag of surrender. The ministers remained inside with the cadets.

At about 11 P.M., guns from a Neva River fortress loosed a barrage of fewer than fifty shells, only two of which hit the Winter Palace, doing little damage. The leaders of the provisional government gave up. The Bolsheviks were in power.

"This skirmish was the Bolshevik November Revolution," summarized Massie, "later magnified in Communist mythology into an epic of struggle and heroism. In fact, life in the capital was largely undisturbed. Restaurants, stores and cinemas on the Nevsky Prospect remained open. Streetcars moved as usual through most of the city, and the ballet performed at the Maryinsky Theater. . . . Nevertheless, this flick of Lenin's finger was all that was necessary to finish Kerensky. . . . When Kerensky left, he carried with him the vanishing dream of a humane, liberal, democratic Russia."[8]

8. Massie, *Nicholas and Alexandra,* pp. 455–456.

7 Lenin and the Workers' State, 1917–1924

THERE was little expectation inside or outside Russia that the Bolsheviks would be able to remain in power long or that the Workers' State would survive. The situation in Russia had as much stability and predictability as a hot pan of popping corn. The Bolsheviks represented only a tiny fraction of the country. In fact, they comprised no more than a minority among the extremists within the Russian socialist parties.

Even Lenin and those closest to him regarded their revolution as nothing more than the opening shot of the uprisings that would follow in other countries, as foreseen by Marx. As Lenin saw it, Russia had been seized in order to create a headquarters for workers' revolutions in industrial countries; an *isolated* socialist revolution in Russia was doomed to failure. In fact, Lenin himself declared in a speech in 1918: "We must not forget that we alone cannot achieve a socialist revolution in one country only, even if it were a less backward country than Russia."

After all, Marx had predicted that revolution would occur first in a highly industrialized country with a big working class. In Russia, however, the working-class revolution had come even though the broad industrial base was but a dim hope for the future. Someone called it Marxism turned upside down.

Events contradicted Lenin and Marx: revolution did *not* erupt elsewhere; yet Russia's revolution *did* survive. It did so in the face of stupendous difficulties. Three particular reasons should be mentioned: First, the Utopian concept of a classless society awakened the idealism of many Russians, especially the young. "Lenin appeared to the young generation," explained Sir Bernard Pares, the British historian who visited Russia many times during the period, "like Moses descending from the mountain with the tablets of the new law, in whose defense no effort seemed too great and no exploit impossible. One of the outstanding features of the revolution, now and later, was the release of energy in the vast masses of the population."

Secondly, the new leadership, when opposed, resorted to a repression as ferocious as any seen under the czars. Thirdly, there was the stamina, flexibility, and brilliant leadership of Lenin. Others played vital roles in this initial period, principally Trotsky; but without Lenin's steady hand, the revolution would not have survived. Even more than *making* the revolution, Lenin's great accomplishment was *preserving* it in spite of civil war, famine, and other catastrophes.

The day after the revolution, November 8, a Bolshevik government was formed. It was called the Soviet of People's Commissars. The chairman was Lenin. Trotsky was commissar of foreign affairs and later commissar for war. Josef Stalin was commissar of nationalities, which meant that his responsibility was the merging of the various national groups in the country.

Lenin became in fact and in deed an absolute dictator. This conformed with Marxist theory: the temporary dictatorship of the proletariat (a dictatorship operated on behalf of the working class) was said to be necessary until all opposition to the revolution disappeared. Where the theory has collapsed, though, is in the *survival* of the *same* form of proletariat dictatorship, somewhat modified and, of course, with different people, to this day.

In the succeeding weeks and months, decisions of tremendous consequence were made.

Lenin in his study in the Kremlin, 1918. *Tass from Sovfoto*

The capital was moved to Moscow because a German army was advancing toward Petrograd. A Red Army of Workers and Peasants was founded to replace the disintegrating military force and to defend the revolution from its opponents. The Bolshevik party changed its name to the Communist party. All private property, including that belonging to foreigners, was confiscated without compensation. All debts to foreign countries incurred by previous Russian governments were repudiated; in other words, the debts would not be paid. In 1924 the country was given the name "Union of Socialist Soviet Republics" (the USSR or, as it is ordinarily called, the Soviet Union).

Negotiations with Germany for peace were opened in December

1917 at Brest-Litovsk (then German, later Polish, it is now Russian and is called Brest). The Treaty of Brest-Litovsk was signed on March 3, 1918, and the Bolsheviks paid a staggering price to obtain peace from the Germans. The former Russian empire was deprived of a fourth of its total arable land and an area in which sixty million people lived. Most of the territory won since the time of Peter the Great was surrendered, including the Ukraine, the Crimea, much of the Caucasus, the Baltic States, Finland, and Poland. Lost were three-quarters of Russia's coal and iron supply, half of its industrial plant, and a quarter of its population.

Lenin had no choice but to accept any terms he could get, no matter how humiliating. The Bolsheviks' own propaganda had caused mass desertions from the army. Only the great distances involved and the battles on the western front had prevented the Germans from marching even deeper into Russia. Lenin had come to power on the promise of peace, but he paid dearly for it (Russia got back a small part of the lost territory after Germany's defeat by the Allied powers in November 1918, and eventually reconquered much of the rest).

Loyal to Marxist principles, Lenin's government immediately handed over the factories to the workers' control. Lenin himself apparently had misgivings about how this might work out; he first asked workers' representatives for assurances that they could operate the factories.

On November 14, a decree was published that placed factories under the direction of workers' committees. The proprietors and managers were not immediately thrown out. Rather, they were placed under the supervision of the elected factory committees, which determined production levels and had access to all correspondence and accounts.

In many cases the workers' actions went far beyond the decree. The owners were ousted. The factory was run by decisions reached at often chaotic meetings of all the workers. It was a heady experiment, but a disastrous one.

The Marxist formula was applied: "From each according to his ability, and to each according to his need." In other words, a worker was supposed to do the very best he could, and his pay would be sufficient to satisfy all his requirements. In practice, it meant that a worker was paid irrespective of the quality of his work; and as a result, less and less work was done. The assurance of a fixed wage, independent of the quality or quantity of one's work, soon reduced production in Russian factories to one-sixth of prerevolution levels. There was a great deal of absenteeism, with workers staying away without good reason.

Since the workers themselves now theoretically owned the factories, Marxists expected that they would safeguard the machinery and other assets. Instead, there was widespread looting by workers of machinery, tools, and manufactured goods.

To bring order out of chaos, the state soon appointed committees of dedicated Communists to manage the factories. In the case of certain heavy industries, organizations known as state trusts were set up to run things. The workers' role as mass managers of industry has been called a "wild experiment," and it was of brief duration.

One of the first decrees issued in November 1917 instituted an eight-hour working day. A shorter working day was prescribed for juveniles, miners and others who worked underground, and those in unhealthy trades. In 1922, these rules were slightly liberalized in one respect: the work day prior to the single day-off was to be only six hours long, with wages being paid as for a full working day. This was an enormous improvement over the ten and twelve hours which, as we have seen, were common in industrial enterprises.

The emancipation of women was accomplished by a decree that provided that men and women workers must receive equal treatment. For Russia this was a genuine revolutionary achievement. However, an obvious motive for the equality of sexes was to broaden the labor force by providing for equal use of men and women; there were few, if any, provisions for protecting women workers, although maternity leaves later became law.

Strikes were declared to be illegal, as they had been under the old regime. The czarist government had outlawed strikes to favor the factory owners and to prevent disorders. The Bolshevik government explained that it was senseless for workers to strike against themselves, since they now owned the plants.

In April 1917, Lenin said that a government official's pay "must not exceed that of a competent workman." This egalitarian principle promptly became law after the revolution; but when Lenin died, it disappeared.

The experiences of workers at a cotton factory near Vladimir, about 125 miles from Moscow, were shared at other plants during the years immediately following the revolution. The founder of the cotton factory and the other executives fled. The herd of laborers tried to form itself into a self-governing community. A skilled worker was elected manager. One of the first tasks was to install electricity in the workers' barracks, where "each family had for its dwelling a narrow though lofty cell (one cannot call it a room), lighted by a tiny window high in the wall. Often as many as seven or eight pairs of lungs inhabited these cells, and the allowance of space was supposed to be seven cubic feet for each person. . . . The sanitary arrangements were unspeakable."[1] A workers' council was established, and it ruled that not more than three persons should occupy each cramped cell. Construction was begun on new quarters.

The worker-managers went to work laying drains to improve the sanitary conditions. Nurseries and kindergartens were organized. The facilities were primitive, but relatively clean; and the teachers were kindly. The existing school was put on two shifts, with classes for the children during the day and adult classes in the evening to eliminate illiteracy. Somehow a library of nine hundred books was collected. A small theater was erected, and an amateur choir, band, and dramatic club were organized.

When the civil war (which we will soon describe) drew near the area, oil and coal fuel were cut off; and the people had to gather wood from the forest and peat from nearby bogs. All of the town's horses were mobilized by the Red Army, and the eight hundred men who were not serving in the military forces cut logs and peat

1. Henry Noel Brailsford, *The Russian Workers' Republic* (New York: Harper, 1921), p. 3.

and hauled them in hand-drawn carts. Food was short and closely rationed for long periods of time. The supply of raw cotton was cut off by war and the factory lay idle for many months. When raw materials became available again, the supply was erratic; and the quality of the cotton cloth produced declined.

A journalist summed up the situation in the cotton-factory town in 1920:

> One felt the force of the explosive deed which had shattered an intolerable oppression. One saw at work the creative will which by some miracle of buoyancy and optimism insists on building and constructing, amid hunger and nakedness. One realized sadly that it had created everything but prosperity. One understood in some measure why it had failed, as one counted the tale of workers absent at the front and caught a glimpse, across a thousand miles of railway, of those cotton fields which war had put out of cultivation. Russia has hardly yet begun a Communist economy. She had only struggled to survive amid war, civil war, and blockade.[2]

The visitor to Moscow and Petrograd during the period discussed in this chapter would have seen whitewashed fences covered with slogans of the revolution. The walls of factories carried placards, which announced innumerable lectures for workingmen. In the battle against illiteracy, Petrograd authorities claimed that in a three-month period, adult schools had cut in half the number of illiterates in the city's population.

Theaters and the opera, which previously had been attended exclusively by the upper classes, were now regularly crowded by audiences mainly composed of workers and their families. Even though the populations of both cities had been reduced by the demands of war, the streets were animated and at certain hours even crowded. Surprisingly, since most vehicles had been commandeered by the military, there still were a considerable number of cabs for hire.

Many shops gave the impression of being shut, but a visitor would find after passing a seemingly closed store a half dozen times that the next time people were standing patiently in line at

2. *Ibid.*, p. 10.

the door. The explanation lay in a rather complicated system of ration cards that gave to each working citizen the right to spend a certain sum of money each month on scarce goods. Cloth, crockery, glass, hardware, shoes, and a great many other items were in short supply. Every day the newspapers announced that ration cards bearing certain numbers could be used in certain shops, and some shops that had appeared closed would open for that day. Every labor union had a committee to which a worker could apply for exceptions to the rationing system if he had urgent need of a scarce item and had exhausted his ration. One of the most tightly rationed items was cloth. Shoes were also in very short supply. Even in the Foreign Ministry in Moscow, in one year only 60 percent of the personnel received any footwear at all; and only 30 percent got boots, which are so essential in Russia's deep snows. Soap was a costly luxury, when available. Scarce supplies were distributed first to hospitals, nurseries, and schools.

Railroad tickets also were rationed. Transportation was one of the country's gravest problems. Under the best circumstances, Russia had only enough locomotives to cope with indispensable civilian traffic. But there were not nearly enough to satisfy both military and civilian needs at once.

Those employed in munitions factories, mines, and certain textile factories supplying the army comprised a favored category of worker. These so-called "armored" workers were supposed to receive extra rations of food, but even bread was in short supply. Many people survived only by obtaining food outside the public markets. For example, many workers, especially in the smaller communities, had patches of land on which they grew potatoes and other staples. In schools, children received one, and in some cases two, free meals a day, which provided some relief for hard-pressed workers' families.

Complaint bureaus were established in each community, and workers and others could submit written complaints if they felt they had been wronged by officials. A committee, which included Communists and workers, acted on complaints considered valid.

Living in close quarters, people quarreled frequently over the sharing of living space and the limited amenities.

Free medical service was quickly organized. Doctors were paid on the same scale as the most skilled industrial workers. There was an almost constant and desperate shortage of drugs, disinfectants, and instruments, even clinical thermometers.

In this society of shortages, the guiding principle was to give the children preference in food, clothing, and everything else. A Red Army officer, a baker in civilian life, explained: "We grew up as slaves. The capitalistic system has ruined us, mind and body. This generation is hopeless. You will see the greatness of Russia only when our children grow up, reared in a socialistic society."[3]

On January 10, 1918, a long-awaited assembly convened to draw up a constitution that would contain guarantees of civil rights for workers and other individual Russians. This was a long yearned-for project that had been set in motion by the Kerensky government well before the Bolshevik Revolution. Lenin and the Bolsheviks were in favor of it. Elections for representatives to the assembly were held throughout the country in November 1917.

When the election results were in, the attitude of the Bolsheviks changed. The Bolsheviks won only 175 seats out of 707.

There were several ways to deal with the situation. One was the democratic, parliamentary method of acknowledging the will of the people and letting the majority rule. Another way was to ignore the vote and use superior physical power (which the Bolsheviks now possessed in the soviets and the Red Guard units) to impose the will of the minority on the majority.

Lenin chose the latter alternative.

The assembly was permitted to convene. The chairman was Victor Chernov, minister of agriculture under Kerensky and a founder of the Socialist Revolutionary party (rival of the Bolsheviks). The proceedings of the first day made it clear that a wide gap existed between the points of view of the Bolsheviks and the other parties on many issues.

Even at this early stage, Lenin had no intention of permitting a parliament or a constitution to interfere in the governing of the

3. *Ibid.*, p. 86.

country. The new Russia was to be run by the workers' soviets from the village level right to the top. The workers were to have the predominant vote in the election of the soviets; in the weighted system of balloting, it was to take five peasants' votes to equal one worker's.

On the second day of the constituent assembly, Bolshevik Red Guards moved in and efficiently cleared the hall. The representatives were sent packing.

Opposition to Lenin and the Communists began taking form. General Kornilov, who had escaped from arrest, organized a center of resistance in the south, and czarist officers gravitated to it. Chernov formed another nucleus. Various national groups in the Ukraine, in the Caucasus, and elsewhere that had always been hostile to Russian rule took up arms against the Lenin regime in the hope of achieving independence for their own areas. Large armies were raised. A long and bloody civil war ensued. It lasted from 1917 to 1921. The so-called White Army was led by Admiral Alexander Kolchak against the "Red Army." Kolchak's ultimate defeat caused him to be described as "a reed painted to look like steel."

The fighting ranged over great distances. At the outset, more than 120,000 men were engaged on each side, and the numbers grew. The lines were thin, and bold sweeping tactics by cavalry played a big part. The United States, Britain, France, and Japan landed small expeditionary forces at Murmansk, Archangel, and Vladivostok to help the anti-Communists. For a time, the White Army controlled much more territory than did Lenin's troops. In October 1919, units of the White Army penetrated to within eighteen miles of Petrograd and within 150 miles of Moscow. Brutality was frequent on both sides. Disease claimed many lives. In large areas it was impossible to carry on farming because of the fighting, and famine resulted. Not the least significant factor in the final victory of the Red Army was Trotsky's tireless and brilliant direction.

"It is no exaggeration to say that Trotsky was the one man mainly responsible for victory in the Civil War," in the opinion of

Colonel Ernest Léderrey, a Swiss army officer who was in Russia at the time organizing Red Cross relief. "With his famous train, which from August 1918 on served as his mobile headquarters (he later had two of them), Trotsky claimed to have turned up whenever the situation on some sector of the front appeared critical. In his own words, the train was 'that vital shovelful of coal that keeps a dying fire alive.' It carried, besides a printing press and signaling equipment (including a radio transmitter for direct contact with Moscow), a small number of hand-picked officers capable of organizing new formations on the spot or taking over from commanders who had proved unequal to their task. The train also carried some motorcars, tobacco, boots, and various comforts for the troops."[4]

Russian opponents of Lenin were driven to desperate measures by the dictatorial nature of Lenin's rule, the arbitrary dismissal of the constituent assembly, and the humiliating Treaty of Brest-Litovsk.

On August 30, 1918, members of an opposition party murdered the Petrograd chief of the secret police force organized by Lenin eight months earlier. Known as the Cheka, a contraction of its long Russian name, it was intended to suppress activities aimed against the success of the revolution. In any guise, it was a resurrection of the dread czarist secret police and was equally brutal and repressive.

On the same August day, a Socialist Revolutionary named Dora Kaplan fired a bullet at Lenin. His wound was serious, but he fully recovered. In the Central Lenin Museum in Moscow, a glass case contains the overcoat that Lenin was wearing; and the bullet hole is visible. The woman assassin was seized and jailed.

The immediate Cheka response to the assassination attempt was to take five hundred persons who were in prison on suspicion of antirevolutionary activities and shoot them as "enemies of the working class."

During the difficult years when survival of the Communist

4. Colonel Ernest Léderrey, "The Red Army During the Civil War," in B. H. Liddell Hart, ed., *The Red Army*, p. 43.

Subbotniks working in Moscow around 1920. *Sovfoto*

government hung by a slender thread, persons suspected of counterrevolutionary activities (aimed at restoring the former rulers) were summarily executed.

The civil war had an immediate effect on Lenin's policies. With a war for survival being fought, leniency toward workers had to be abandoned, even though theoretically they were the new owners of industry. Pampering was out. Production was stressed. Production was vital to the war effort.

One instrument to extract the maximum effort from workers was the labor union. Unions gradually ceased to be organizations that represented the workers and became organs of the state. The principle of "One Factory, One Union" was applied everywhere. This meant that every worker in one factory, whatever his occupation, joined the union to which the factory belonged. A report, at the time, of a British trade union delegation to Russia cited an example: in a machine tool factory, not only were the carpenters and bricklayers employed on factory repairs made to join the Metal Workers' Union, but so also were the cooks.

A device to get people to work harder was called the *subbotniki*, or "voluntary Saturdays" of unpaid work, after completion of the regular work time. This began in April 1919, when, according to the *Great Soviet Encyclopedia*, "Communists of the Moscow-Kazan railway sorting depot organized the first Communist *subbotnik*."

Lenin described the event as a "victory over personal inertia, lack of discipline, petty-bourgeois egoism, over all those habits which accursed capitalism has bequeathed to us." The extra day of work without pay does not appear to have been quite as voluntary as was made out. There was a good deal of organizing behind the scenes by members of the Communist party, which was purposely kept small in number in order to assure a tightly controlled, disciplined, and dedicated leadership class.

The *subbotniki* phenomenon lasted for about a year and soon died out. The emphasis on worker discipline continued unabated.

In November 1919, Lenin declared that "those, who in spite of repeated injunctions, demands, and orders, continue to avoid work should be punished with merciless severity." Comrades' disciplinary courts were created. These were the civilian equivalent of the military courts that were functioning in the Red Army to maintain troop discipline.

The problem was to keep workers at their machines. The new liberty was an exhilarating experience. Workers, free to seek jobs where they wished, were moving from factory to factory in search of the best pay and conditions. This was interfering with output. It was made an offense.

Workers who "willfully" left enterprises were considered "labor deserters." Absenteeism and lateness at work were declared punishable offenses.

A court consisted of three members—one from the Communist party's managers of the plant, one from the trade unions (an agency of the Communist party), and one from among the factory's workers. The penalties at the disposal of the courts included: public reprimand; up to a month's reduced pay; assignment to "hard, socially useful labor" with "appropriate pay." Particularly obstructive workers were sent to concentration camps for six months.

Lenin spoke again on the subject of discipline among workers on April 1920 at a congress of the Communist party. To raise labor productivity to the utmost, said Lenin, there would be no hesitancy "to use coercion, since no revolution was ever made without coercion, and the proletariat has the right to use coercion to hold its own at any cost . . . iron discipline is necessary."

The slogan became "He Who Does Not Work, Neither Shall He Eat."

The end of the civil war found Russia exhausted and near ruin. From firsthand experience in Russia at the time, Sir Bernard Pares described the situation:

> Fantastic inflation and hopeless deficits marked the abandonment of all conventional principles of exchange. Industry was more than five-sixths gone, which in an industrial country would have meant the final ruin of the whole project. Transport had worn out most of its existing reserves and, in the failure of repair and production, except for military purposes it had broken down almost completely. . . . The fact that lay at the bottom of all other facts was that during the Civil War productive work had almost stopped, and that the country was living on its reserves from a previous period. . . .
>
> For the most part the peasants ceased to produce any more than they consumed. This meant famine for the towns, whose population fell with the most alarming rapidity. That of the abandoned capital, Petrograd, went down to one third. Town markets became so empty that even dogs and pigeons stopped coming to them, and town-dwellers made long railway journeys to find peasants who could give them food in return for boots, clothes, or other articles. As all such trade was illegal, the traveller was liable to see his hard-won supply taken from him before he could get back home.[5]

A great drought added to the misery. Cases of cannibalism were reported. A terrible epidemic of malaria spread. About 5 million people died of starvation. Very considerable assistance was given

5. Pares, *A History of Russia*, pp. 506–507.

to the suffering people by the American Relief Administration, led by Herbert Hoover, who later became president of the United States.

In March 1921, dissatisfaction with Lenin's dictatorship found violent expression. Sailors at the naval base at Kronstadt, on the Gulf of Finland, mutinied against their officers. It was a reflection of the widespread bitterness at the failure of communism to provide the promised freedoms and material advantages. The mutiny was stamped out with great vengeance.

Lenin recognized that the emergency conditions cried out for emergency measures. He was prepared to sacrifice principles temporarily to save the regime. During the first part of 1921, he put into effect the so-called New Economic Policy, which was generally referred to as the NEP. It was a retreat on the economic front from the principles and ideals of Marxism. The purpose was to buy breathing space. Neither Lenin nor anyone else in the Communist hierarchy thought for a moment of abandoning their Marxist aims permanently. But the immediate need was to increase the volume of production at whatever the cost to ideology.

The NEP was a partial return in the economic arena to capitalism, pure and simple. The objective was to bring into play again the personal initiative and drive (the Communists would call it "greed") that goes with private ownership.

Smaller factories were, for the most part, handed over to individual owners to run for profit, and they paid rent to the state. The ban on private ownership of shops, which had been imposed immediately after the revolution, was lifted. The government, resigned to the reality that *world* revolution was not in the cards for the foreseeable future, turned eagerly to capitalist countries for trade and business deals.

A bourgeois class was restored in Russia.

An excellent summary of what transpired during the period of the NEP is given by Harry Schwartz:

> Private trade was once again permitted, and a new class of retail merchants sprang up immediately in all areas of the economy, quickly dominating retail distribution and playing a very important role as wholesalers.

Illegal private trade had existed during War [the civil war] Communism, when thousands of "bagmen" trudged between city and country, bartering food for consumer goods and playing a significant role in what limited exchange of goods took place.

During 1922–23, about 75 percent of the retail trade volume of the Soviet Union was accounted for by private merchants; state and cooperative stores did only about 15 and 10 percent of the business, respectively.

In industry, too, the state relinquished some of its former primacy, keeping the largest and most important factories and branches of industry, but leasing many smaller plants to cooperatives and private operators and restoring others to their original owners.

Foreign concessionaires were allowed to take over some enterprises. . . .

A study published in 1923 found that only 8.5 percent of all industrial enterprises in the USSR belonged to the government; but these employed over 84 percent of all industrial workers, indicating clearly the small and often minuscule size of cooperative and privately run enterprises.[6]

Capitalistic incentives were given to the peasants to encourage them to raise larger crops. The government abandoned its practice of requisitioning grain without payment.

The NEP brought with it a short-lived amelioration of the workers' lot. A total of sixteen holidays a year was set in 1922. These included: January 1, New Year's Day; January 22 (the anniversary of "Bloody Sunday" in 1905); March 12 (the overthrow of czarist autocracy in 1917); May 1 (International Labor Day); November 7 (the Bolshevik Revolution). Lenin's death on January 21, 1924, was thereafter commemorated on January 22, along with "Bloody Sunday."

The despised comrades' disciplinary courts were abolished under the NEP, and they were replaced in September 1924 by a set of regulations called Rules of Internal Labor Order. The new rules guaranteed the worker freedom to change his job if he wished. As in any privately owned plant in capitalist countries, the factory manager was given authority, within limits, to impose penalties for absenteeism and similar shortcomings.

6. Schwartz, *Russia's Soviet Economy*, p. 107.

During the seven years that the NEP lasted, it brought remarkable results, testifying to the effectiveness of the tried and true profit motive, ideological considerations aside. The peasants produced bigger harvests. There was a marked revival of light industry, and consumer goods became more plentiful. Heavy industry, still run principally by the government, continued to lag; and there were some unemployment and worker dissatisfaction. This caused Lenin to declare at a Communist congress in November 1922:

> The salvation of Russia lies not only in a good harvest on the peasant farms—that is not enough; and not only in the good condition of light industry, which provides the peasants with consumer goods—this too is not enough; we also need *heavy* industry . . . without heavy industry we shall be doomed as an independent country.

The goal of a buildup of heavy industry had to wait for Lenin's successor.

Lenin's expediency in returning to a modified form of capitalism in the NEP drew scorn from Winston Churchill:

> Lenin was the Grand Repudiator. He repudiated everything. He repudiated God, King, Country, morals, treaties, debts, rents, interest, the laws and customs of centuries, all contracts written or implied, the whole structure—such as it is—of human society. In the end he repudiated himself. He repudiated the Communist system.[7]

The NEP was the last achievement of Lenin's life. Exhausted, drained to the dregs from revolution and war, he suffered a stroke in the spring of 1922. A second stroke in 1923 deprived him of speech. He spent the last years of his life in a rambling, two-story white house with a portico of six Doric columns twenty-three miles south of Moscow. It is now a national museum.

A special double banister was installed to enable Lenin to support himself with both hands on the staircase following partial paralysis from the strokes. Under the staircase stands Lenin's battery-driven car, by which he propelled himself around the extensive grounds. An antique movie projector stands on a table in a large sun-room.

Lenin slept in a room of Spartan simplicity on a cot-sized bed.

7. Churchill, *The Aftermath*, p. 75.

His desk, oddly enough, stood in his wife's comparatively spacious connecting bedroom. A rose-colored glass screen separated his wife's bed from the rest of the room.

The rooms are filled with memorabilia of Lenin's last years— letters, documents, edicts, manuscripts, and photographs. A white plaster mask of Lenin made after his death rests on a table.

Lenin died in 1924. The extent to which he had captured the loyalty and devotion of the Russian masses was manifest at his funeral. Walter Duranty, an American correspondent in Moscow at the time, wrote: "Three-quarters of a million people waited an average of five hours in the Arctic cold of thirty degrees below zero, night and day alike, before passing through the hall where Lenin's body lay in state."

As so frequently in the past at the demise of a Russian leader, there lurked the suspicion that an impatient rival's hand had hastened the end. The suspected individual was Josef Stalin.

8 The Stalin Era, 1924–1953

LENIN'S second stroke left him completely incapable of governing the country. In the months before his death, the struggle for succession began. One contender, Leon Trotsky, later wrote that Lenin was fatally poisoned by Stalin, the general secretary of the Central Committee of the Communist party. This unproved accusation has been cause for contention among historians ever since.

In one way or another, Stalin eliminated all of his rivals and soon emerged as the absolute and undisputed dictator. He was the first ruler of Communist Russia who came from a working-class family. His father was a shoemaker; and his mother, a peasant.

Born in 1879 in the Caucasian mountain town of Gori, in the region of Georgia, Stalin's real name was Josef Vissarionovich Dzhugashvili. From the time he was nineteen years old until the revolution in 1917, he lived the harried and uncertain life of a full-time revolutionary terrorist. Before that, from the age of fourteen, he had studied for the priesthood; he was thrown out of the seminary for revolutionary activities.

He took the conspirative name of Stalin, which means "made of steel"; and it was apt. The legend is that his comrades suggested the name in tribute to his iron durability and immovable will. Stalin once told American journalist Walter Duranty that he believed in only one thing, "the power of the human will." It was written of him that "He is about as emotional as a slab of basalt. If he has nerves, they are veins in rock."

When he became ruler of the Soviet Union, Stalin was to apply his steely characteristics to the construction of factories on a massive scale, completely transforming the face of the country. He set himself to the task without regard for human life or suffering. Stalin's explanation was that "you cannot make a revolution with silk gloves."

Between 1902 and 1913, Stalin was arrested five times by the czarist police and escaped each time. It is said that in 1906 he took part in a bank robbery in Tiflis, the Georgian capital, in order to replenish the funds of the underground organization.

Unlike Lenin, Trotsky, and other prominent revolutionaries, Stalin did not choose prolonged exile abroad, but remained in the country to wage constant clandestine warfare against the czars. In 1911 he founded *Pravda* ("Truth") as an illegal newspaper; it is still published, now as the official daily of the Communist party. In 1913 he was arrested and exiled for life to northern Siberia, where he remained until the March 1917 overthrow of Czar Nicholas II. Then he hurried back to Petrograd, joined Lenin, and became a leading figure in the proletariat dictatorship.

The feud between Stalin and Trotsky was unrelenting. Stalin gradually gained the upper hand. In 1929, he ordered Trotsky to leave the USSR; most countries refused to accept him. Angrily protesting to the last, Trotsky was finally pushed across the frontier into Turkey, which had agreed to grant him asylum. Later, he received permission to move to France, then to Norway, and finally to Mexico. He was a prolific writer and kept up a constant barrage of criticism and abuse of Stalin from his places of exile. Undoubtedly, he left supporters and perhaps an underground organization in the Soviet Union. In August 1940, at his home near Mexico City, he was murdered with a pickaxe. It was driven into his skull by a Belgian-born Iranian believed to have been sent by Stalin.

It is instructive to consider the simple working-class origins of the man who stood at the pinnacle of Soviet power from 1924 until 1953. The word *gori* means "small mountain," and Stalin's native town was named for a nearby elevation. Gori is a grayish, dusty community on a broad plateau backed by green, steep ridges. Stalin was born and lived for four years in a room rented by his parents.

In 1935 the small house was converted into a museum. Stalin's mother was still alive, and she helped restore their room to the condition of his childhood. Stalin and his parents slept in a narrow single bed. The other furnishings in the small room were a crude wooden table, four low square stools, two plain chests, a samovar, and a wall mirror flanked by two candleholders. A box contained the father's cobbling tools. Who can say how much this early environment of poverty contributed to the severity of Stalin's dictatorship?

Lenin's great contribution was to *make* the revolution and cling to it in spite of fantastic difficulties. Stalin's great contribution was to make a *success* of the state created by the revolution. More than any man since Peter the Great, Stalin devoted his life to eliminating Russian backwardness.

He once said: "The history of old Russia is of defeats due to backwardness. She was beaten by the Mongol Khans. She was beaten by the Turkish Beys. She was beaten by the Swedish feudal lords. She was beaten by the Polish-Lithuanian squires. She was beaten by the Anglo-French imperialists. She was beaten by the Japanese barons. All beat her for her backwardness, her military backwardness, her cultural backwardness, her governmental backwardness, her industrial backwardness, her agricultural backwardness."

Stalin was convinced that the most important step in ending Russia's backwardness was to build up her industry. This would have two effects, he said. First, it would make the Soviet Union immune to possible attack from capitalist countries. Secondly, it would demonstrate the superiority of the Communist system over capitalism and thereby stimulate the revolutions, predicted by Marx, which had so far failed to materialize in other countries.

In short, behind industrialization stood the determination to build an unconquerable, self-sufficient fortress, which would be absolutely safe from outside attack and which could itself develop into a springboard for the expansion of Communist power into the rest of the outside world.

Stalin's insistence on industrialization followed a theme expressed by Lenin, who had said that "we are doomed as a civilized state—let alone as a socialist state" without heavy industry. But Lenin had counted on the freely given help of industrialized countries, which, he hopefully anticipated, would fall by revolution into the hands of the workers.

What made Stalin's program novel and dramatic was its grandiose scope and his intention to go it alone, to achieve the goals without help from other governments. His goal was to overtake and surpass, by Russia's own unassisted energies, the most advanced countries of the capitalist world.

The attainment of the goal was all the more difficult because, except for the minority class of factory workers, there was only an army of unskilled and mostly ignorant peasant labor available. The cost in human suffering and in human lives was great, but the essentials of the goal were reached. Russia did not, by any means, surpass the highly developed capitalist states at that time, but massive industrialization *was* achieved by Stalin.

To accomplish this, in 1928 he inaugurated the first in a series of five-year plans. The publicity given to it and the curiosity it generated everywhere made the Five-Year Plan a household word throughout the world.

The First Five-Year Plan and those that followed can most simply be described as economic timetables. Detailed and precise goals were set for each sector of the economy. The use of every national resource, whether coal or iron ore or human beings, was carefully prescribed. The aim was to take the element of chance out of the economy by deciding well in advance what would be produced, where, and in what quantities. It contained more than a blueprint for the rapid expansion of *industrial* production. It also included plans for increasing agricultural output and for the construction of schools, hospitals, and apartments. Not a single aspect of economic activity was overlooked.

Every industry has a production target, and so does agriculture. It is readily understood how a target can be set for the number of trees to be felled by the timber industry or the number of pipe lengths to be manufactured. But without first consulting the fish, it may be difficult to see how Soviet fishermen can be assigned a precise number of fish to catch. Yet under the five-year plans they are. By taking into consideration the catch of previous seasons and the availability of new equipment, a catch quota is set. This is done, too, for whales. Russia sends a whaling expedition to Antarctic waters each season for about seven months. The flotilla has in recent years had as its quota the blubber of one thousand whales, which it usually brings back.

On December 31, 1932, it was announced that the First Five-Year Plan had been fulfilled ahead of schedule in four and a quarter years. The figures released showed, however, that the plan's goals had not been achieved in all departments. It was an uneven performance. Failures in one area were balanced by unexpectedly good results in another. While the output of machinery and electrical equipment, for example, had exceeded the goal by 57 percent, heavy metallurgy production was 33 percent short of the target. The aim for steel production capacity had been 10,400,000 tons, but the output in 1932 was under 6 million tons. The minimal targets set for consumer goods had fallen short by more than 25 percent.

The Second Five-Year Plan was promptly put into effect, and successive five-year plans after it. Each plan called for total mobilization and regimentation.

Great demands were placed on the Russian worker. The notoriously low standard of living fell further and reached the barest subsistence level. Factories cut back sharply on the manufacture of consumer goods. Items of everyday use that are normally taken for granted—household furniture, pots and pans, suits, shirts, dresses, toothbrushes—were in scarce supply. Many items were strictly rationed.

Factories were established in the wilderness to the east, in the Ural Mountains and in Siberia to be close to the mines furnishing raw materials. New industrial communities (more in the nature of encampments than cities) sprang up. People were uprooted from

A workers' meeting in a Moscow factory during the Stalin era. *USSR Magazine from Sovfoto*

the rural areas and worked, often half-starved, and in winter half-frozen, in the primitive settlements.

The constant emphasis was on increasing and speeding up production. The pace was brutal. An example of the trend was the progressive reduction in the number of annual holidays from sixteen, to ten, and then to six. The average worker was required to spend an inordinate amount of time at lectures that were a combination of indoctrination and exhortation. Workers were expected to cheer the mention of Stalin's name.

Workers gradually gained in skill and, according to one foreign foreman in a Moscow tool factory in 1937, "the average present-day mechanic was 25 percent more efficient than his predecessor thirty years ago, and also he was more intelligent and took more interest in his work. The younger men and women were always eager to learn more and to turn out better quality as well as greater quantity."[1]

The same writer recorded other impressions:

I entered the factory dining-hall, which was lofty, clean, had facilities for personal tidying up, and was filled with a smell that gave one

1. Silver, *The Russian Workers' Own Story*, pp. 60–61.

hope of a good dinner. Opposite the entrance the wall was adorned with portraits of Marx, Lenin and Stalin, with slogans, propaganda posters and many diagrams. There were also three large blackboards to each of which was attached a wall-newspaper, which contained news and correspondence of interest to this particular factory only, and a leading article . . . ending with: "Thanks to the clear guidance of our great leader Comrade Stalin. . . ."

In the dining-halls, workers' clubs and in all other public places in Moscow, people must have shared my opinion that "Moscow swarms with spies." While the loudspeakers, newspapers and cinemas were working overtime trying to impress on the people the great importance . . . of "our great leader Comrade Stalin," people generally seemed more than ever inclined to confine talk to ordinary personal affairs. . . .

Only one reckless fellow I encountered in a restaurant dared to comment on a propagandist lecture. . . . He lifted his right hand and lowered it three times, each time saying slowly: "Stalin, Stalin, Stalin again!" then continued: "I guess things must be wrong somewhere or that the Kremlin crowd is smitten by some nervous disease. I will ask you a question, my fair and enlightened comrade, does your party believe that people will accept any animal as a lion because thousands of asses . . . go about braying 'Lion, Lion?' I think they would rather suspect an ass in a lion's skin. Was it ever found necessary to run about proclaiming Lenin a lion? People merely had to understand Lenin and they admired him automatically."

The attitude of a middle-aged worker toward the new order was conveyed in a conversation with the above-mentioned writer in an Odessa park: "I've been a workman all my life," said the Russian, "and so was my father. It is true that I was compelled to serve three years in the czar's army, but I did it quite unwillingly. During the war I bribed the doctor to certify me as unfit. It is true that, as a specially skilled bootmaker, I used to make boots for high officials, but I did it not because I liked them, but because they paid me high prices. You said that Russia now belongs to the proletariat, but I don't know which part of it belongs to me or to my children, who are also workers. Before the revolution I did know which part of Russia belonged to me, for I could point out a little house and shop which even the czar himself could not have taken away from me. Now I am only allowed to occupy one room in that very house, and three of us, all grown-up people, have to live in it, and have to pay rent for the right to live in a room in the house for which I worked and saved for five and twenty years."[2]

It was during Stalin's Second Five-Year Plan that the pressure on workers to speed up their efforts reached a peak. It was then that the Stakhanovite movement was launched. A Stakhanovite was a worker who dramatically exceeded his norm (that is, the amount of production that was expected of him in a day). The word "Stakhanovite" came from the name of Alexei Stakhanov, a coal miner who managed, during a work shift in August 1935, to exceed by seven times the normal amount of coal extracted. He cut 102 tons of coal and overnight, through the propaganda efforts of the Communist press, became a national hero.

Stakhanov's accomplishment was the result of careful planning. He arranged beforehand to have someone immediately replenish the supply of compressed air for his pneumatic drill when necessary. Two workers, known as timberers, were assigned exclusively to him, propping up the shaft with timber to prevent cave-ins as soon as he had finished cutting a section. Arrangements were made for other miners to stay out of Stakhanov's way during his record-breaking day.

By disregarding his assistants' contributions and ascribing the output entirely to him, the authorities made Stakhanov's record seem much more impressive than in fact it was.

With prodding from Communist party activists, the idea spread to other industries. It was not an automatic thing. The *Great Soviet Encyclopedia* concedes that the Communist party "from the very start calculated correctly that the Stakhanovite movement could not develop spontaneously, and it needed leadership and assistance." This was provided. In November 1935, Stalin himself presided at the opening session of a conference in the Kremlin honoring Stakhanovites from all over the country. They were

2. *Ibid.,* pp. 65, 66, 84–85.

awarded a medal known as the Order of Lenin. Later, a special award called "Hero of Socialist Labor" was bestowed on exemplary workers. They were also given sums of money as prizes.

Not everyone was pleased by the Stakhanovites' accomplishments. For most workers the setting of new records simply meant that the amount of nuts or bolts or coal they would be expected to produce in a day would be raised. The murders of "leading shockworkers," apparently by indignant co-workers, were reported in Soviet newspapers. It was necessary to issue a decree ordering "severe punishment" of persons found guilty of "sabotage of Stakhanovite methods of work."

A Communist party official was obliged to warn: "The party will not shrink from any measures that will help sweep away all opponents from the victorious path of the Stakhanovite movement." Court cases were reported in the press where sentences of

Alexei Stakhanov. *Tass from Sovfoto*

two to four years "deprivation of liberty" were given to opponents of the Stakhanovite speedup.

The poignant complaint of a metal worker was contained in a letter published by the newspaper *Trud* ("Labor") on July 3, 1929:

> Present-day working conditions are called "sweating." . . . Who are these record-breaking workers? Young Communists, youth full of strength and zeal. With thát, of course, you can move mountains. And their example is imitated by reckless oldsters who may once in a while succeed in a record performance. But how long can they last? One month, two months, maybe six months. . . . But we are just ordinary workers and have to work for years to come.

There was more than honor involved in being a Stakhanovite. Higher wages were involved. Workers were paid by piecework—and in many cases still are—at a standard rate for each unit produced. A worker's wages depended on his actual output.

As early as 1918, Lenin, writing of the need to "increase the productivity of labor," had proposed that each worker be paid according to the number of hinges or springs he produced, or the number of bricks he laid, or the number of peaches canned.

This system of payment went into effect in 1919 and was steadily expanded to include as many fields of endeavor as possible. This, of course, was a departure from Lenin's original intention that everyone should be paid the same wage; his idealistic concept did not work in practice. As Stalin was later to explain, "The consequence of wage equalization is that the unskilled worker lacks the incentive to become a skilled worker. . . . We cannot tolerate a situation where a rolling-mill hand in a steel mill earns no more than a sweeper."

By 1931 about half the total man-hours worked were paid on piece rates. By 1955 almost three-quarters of the workers in industry were on piecework. As automated processes were introduced into industry, the proportion of pieceworkers decreased and by 1970 had fallen to between 40 and 50 percent of all workers.

Basically, the piecework system operates like this: for each type of work a norm is set. The norm may be changed from time to time as, for example, when new methods or machinery are introduced or when the workers start exceeding the norm regularly. The worker who exactly fulfills the norm in his work, say, in a textile factory receives the basic wage for his job. Once the norm is fulfilled, the worker's wage rises substantially with each additional bolt of cloth taken from the machines under his care. If the worker produces fewer bolts of cloth than the norm, his pay is reduced proportionately.

Under this system there is no guarantee of a *minimum* wage, a deplorable condition by Western labor standards.

If a worker fails to achieve his norm because of a machinery breakdown that is not his fault, he suffers nevertheless. He is usually paid a minimum of two-thirds of his wage rate.

When a number of workers are responsible for turning out a single product, as in most assembly lines, the so-called "brigade piecework system" is used. Here a norm is set for the brigade as a whole, and brigade piece rates are paid accordingly. The brigades' income is divided up among the brigade workers in proportion to their skills.

The experience of one worker on piece rates in the early 1950s was related by an American correspondent in Moscow:

A very great deal of Russian industry is operated on a piecework, bonus-for-production-above-norm basis. It is not unlike the . . . system which American labor unions have so bitterly and persistently fought. And with the pressure on Soviet factory directors to "make the planned profit" the temptation to sweat labor is irresistible. I was told once by a man named Victor who worked in a shoe factory that several times he managed to raise his wages to a very respectable level, say 1,800 to 2,000 rubles [$450 to $500 at the official exchange rate at that time] a month, by producing above the norm for his job. But after a month or two of such production the factory supervisor came along, revalued his norm (always upward) and he found himself cut back to the 800 or 900 [$200 or $225] he was making before. Or even lower if he was unable to maintain the new high production level.

Victor with his eight hundred rubles a month was earning about the average wage for the Moscow area. . . . Victor and the others like him received their eight hundred rubles for a forty-eight hour week, a six-day eight-hour shift (which they often worked in the form of two twenty-four hour shifts, a highly uneconomic and inefficient procedure but one which enables many workers to hold down two jobs, sleeping half the time on both of them). Thus, Victor earned a little more than four rubles [$1] an hour.[3]

Ten percent of Victor's pay was deducted for purchase of state savings bonds. Later, the figure was lowered to 5 percent. The deduction was described as "voluntary," but, in fact, the worker had no choice in the matter. The bonds run fifteen years and pay no interest; periodic drawings are held for lottery cash prizes paid to bond-holders. Victor once won 200 rubles [$50], but he knew a man who had won 10,000 [$2,500].

Stalin's five-year plans required further tightening of labor discipline. In March 1927, the Rules of Internal Labor Order, mentioned in the previous chapter, were amended to provide more stringent punishment of absentee workers. For instance, three days' absence without good reason in any one month became punishable by dismissal without notice. By November 1932, the penalties were increased; and for even one day's unauthorized absence, a worker could be dismissed, deprived of his rights to use food ration cards, or evicted from the living space allotted to him by the factory.

Moral and economic pressures were now applied to "floaters," workers who changed jobs. So-called courts of honor were set up in workshops and factories to judge workers, and the names of "floaters" were displayed on bulletin boards to shame them. "A lengthy period at the same factory" was one of the conditions made for priority in housing, for free entrance to higher education, for admission to vacation-resort establishments, and for rations of scarce goods. In key industries an extra three days' annual leave was given to those with two or more years' service in one factory. Even the payment of sickness benefits was limited to workers with three years' service. The epithet of "disorganizer of production"

3. Harrison Salisbury, *American in Russia* (New York: Harper, 1955), pp. 225–226.

was applied to anyone who left his job without notice or changed jobs more than once a year, even with notice.

In 1932 a document known as the "internal passport" was introduced better to control the movement of workers. On applying for work, the employee had to produce this passport and have his place of work entered in it. A primary objective was to prevent workers from leaving vital factories for better paying jobs on crash-program construction sites. *Pravda* said that the internal passport helped control "floaters" and "money-grabbers."

These government measures to extract the maximum production from the Russian worker were accompanied by a genuine effort to improve the quality of his life in some respects.

Education was made compulsory and free; gradually, ten years of schooling were provided in cities and seven years in many country areas. A complete system of state insurance eventually covered accidents, old age, and disabilities incurred at work. Unemployment was declared to have been abolished; and although this was an exaggeration, the fact is that there were jobs for almost everyone.

Considerable strides were made in upgrading the quality and availability of free medical care. In this field the Russian worker's lot has shown great improvement. In a letter written in 1913 Lenin advised Maxim Gorky, the novelist and playwright, to avoid doctors of the revolutionary party: "But really, in ninety-nine cases out of a hundred, doctor-comrades are asses. . . . To try on yourself the discoveries of a Bolshevik—that's terrifying." In saying this, Lenin recognized that a physician who was attracted to the early radical Bolshevik political theories might be radical in his practice of medicine as well. (At present, of course, a physician is not necessarily a member of the small Communist party any more than the average factory worker is.)

When the Bolsheviks took power in 1917, notes a study of Soviet medicine, "the regime's very existence and security were threatened by deteriorating health conditions aggravated by the lack of medical personnel, supplies, and facilities. In particular, the regime's stability was seriously endangered by a series of epidemics which found fertile ground among an already ill-nourished and weakened population; epidemics, furthermore, which could not be checked because of the lack of soap and other disinfectants."[4]

The figures for typhus, for example, are terrifying. In 1913 there were 7.3 cases registered per ten thousand people. In 1918 the figure was 21.9 cases. The number of persons afflicted took a tremendous leap the following year when it reached 265.3, and the climb continued; the all-time high was in 1920 with 393.9 Russians of every ten thousand suffering from typhus. In addition, there were epidemics of smallpox, dysentery, scarlet fever, measles, and malaria.

Speaking to a congress of soviets in 1919, Lenin, referring to the carrier of typhus, declared: "Either the louse defeats socialism or socialism defeats the louse."

Socialism won. Within six months of the Bolshevik Revolution, the new regime had set up a central medical organization headed by trusted Communists with ample powers. "Medical education was thrown open to those classes of the population that had been largely barred from it in the prerevolutionary days—the workers, the peasants, the minorities. A deliberate effort was made to keep the children of the former 'exploiting' classes from entering the medical faculties; not only did they have last choice, but they were made to pay tuition while the others received their education free and were provided with living stipends."[5]

Medical services available to the population rapidly increased. The number of hospital beds increased in the cities from 93,200 to 168,500 and almost as much in the rural areas. The incidence rate for typhus dropped steadily to a reassuring 4 per 10,000 people in 1927.

A good yardstick of progress is the number of physicians. In the period 1913–1928, for example, the number of physicians more than tripled. In 1913 there were about 28,000 doctors and dentists in the area now constituting the USSR. This figure rose to 155,000 in 1940,

4. Mark G. Field, *Doctor and Patient in Soviet Russia* (Cambridge, Mass.: Harvard University Press, 1957).

5. *Ibid.*

265,031 in 1950, and 333,776 in 1955, just after the end of the Stalin era.

Horrendous purges took place during Stalin's reign. It has been said that Stalin was responsible for more deaths than any man in history, with the possible exceptions of Hitler and Genghis Khan.

Many old Bolsheviks were arrested, imprisoned, and tortured, and eventually surprised the world by abjectly pleading guilty in open court. These included close colleagues of Lenin and of Stalin, men who fought in the revolution and some of the most famous names of Russian communism's early days. Every possible rival to Stalin was executed or imprisoned. A sheaf of charges was brought against the accused men—conspiracy to overthrow the Soviet government, to murder Stalin, to sabotage industry, to restore capitalism.

The purge extended to the highest army officers and finally to the head of the secret police himself. He was replaced by a fellow-Georgian of Stalin's named Laurenti Beria: it was a name to remember.

Thousands of lesser officials were purged too. The downfall of each famous personage resulted in the arrest of hundreds of insignificant people who at one time or another had been associated with him. Many managers of industries were among the victims condemned to death, imprisonment, or concentration camps. This nightmare period, which Russia has not yet forgotten, came to an end with the last trials in 1939.

The result was a frightened, intimidated country totally in Stalin's grip.

According to Soviet doctrine, of course, the industrial workers of the USSR constitute the ruling class of the country. But the people who actually have run the country since the 1917 revolution have been the members of the Communist party. Stalin totally dominated the party.

The policy from Lenin's time to the present has been to keep the Communist party a small, select group of people of proven loyalty. Only a small fraction of the industrial workers could belong.

At the time of the 1917 Revolution, the party claimed to have about 200,000 members; in 1938 its membership had grown to 2,300,000; and at the end of World War II, in 1945, there were about 6 million. Along with population growth, the party membership increased to over 14 million in 1970. Although varying from period to period, the Communist party, generally speaking, has comprised less than 4 percent of the population.

From the beginning, members of the party were insinuated into every activity in city and country. Loyal Communists run the factories or look over the managers' shoulder. They also control the trade unions, which, as we have noted, have as their main function to see that labor policies set by the Communist party are carried out at the factory level.

Lenin is supposed to have remarked once with engaging candor that there could be any number of political parties in the Soviet Union but only on one condition. The Communist party must be in power, and all the other parties must be in jail.

The terrible toll of the purges was surpassed by the even more fearful toll taken by Stalin's forced-collectivization program. This was part of the First Five-Year Plan. The farmers were ordered to give up their individual land holdings. The land was then grouped into larger collective and state farms.

Stalin's aim was to grow larger crops for export through mechanized farming of vast areas than was possible on the uneconomically small holdings of the individual peasants. By 1933 some twenty-five million individual peasant holdings were concentrated into large collective and state farms, but at a shocking price.

The peasants resisted tenaciously. For generations they had fought for possession of land. They would not readily surrender what had been acquired through the 1917 revolution. Rather than cooperate with the government and turn their cattle over to joint ownership, many peasants chose to kill the animals.

It is estimated that almost 50 percent of the farm animals in the country were slaughtered. For a quarter century or more thereafter, the production of livestock in the USSR did not make up for this catastrophic depletion.

At first Communist party functionaries tried persuasion on the farmers. When this proved unavailing, millions of peasants who owned a few horses or cows were wiped out as a class. R. D. Charques provides a vivid description: "The killings, the rounding-up of groups of obdurate peasants by machine-gun squads, were warnings only. Droves of peasants—sometimes the population of entire villages—were packed off in thousands from all parts of Russia to forced labor and semi-starvation in the mines, timber camps, and construction projects of the east or the Arctic north."

The tragedy did not end there. Farmers refused to harvest their grain, most of which was to be turned over to the government. The peasants gambled that by passive resistance they would overcome Stalin's will. Rather than see the crops rot in the fields and the farmer die of starvation, Stalin would relent in his plans for collectivization. So they thought. They were wrong. Stalin did not move a finger to save the crops or the peasants and perhaps five million people died of starvation in this man-made famine. It has been said that first the peasants killed their animals; then they killed themselves.

The incalculable human misery did, however, produce the results that Stalin sought. Between 1926 and 1940 the output of Soviet industries increased 900 percent—an astounding figure. This obviously entailed an enormous expansion of the labor force. The number of workers (persons employed outside of agriculture) swelled rapidly.

In 1924, at the time of Lenin's death, the labor force totaled 5,843,000. Stalin's immediate emphasis on industrialization raised the number of workers to 9,545,000 in 1928, when the First Five-Year Plan started. By 1940 the number of workers of all sorts had risen to 31,200,000.

When Stalin's intensive industrialization program began, Russia had a sizable corps of competent technical personnel of all kinds, but not enough to achieve the rapid pace that he sought. It was necessary to seek foreign help. The employment of foreigners continued until the purges in the mid-1930s, when official suspicion toward the outside world became rampant. The Communist leaders turned to the West for technically trained personnel as had

A general view in 1940 of a factory district in Gorky (now Novgorod), showing the results of Stalin's massive industrialization plans. *Tass from Sovfoto*

the czars before them. Much of the advanced machinery required
in the vital first stages of an economic development program were
purchased from private firms in Britain, Germany, the United
States. During most of the 1920s and 1930s, large numbers of
American, British, French, German, and other foreign technicians
were brought to the USSR to superintend the construction of new
plants, mines, and dams. They introduced new production processes and instructed Russians in technical skills.

The great Dnieper River hydroelectric system, for example, was
built under the supervision of Americans; its original giant trans-
formers were bought from United States companies.

A significant number of young Russians were sent abroad, as in
the time of Peter the Great, to study in foreign schools and to take
jobs in foreign factories, where they could learn advanced Western
technology.

In 1939 the war that was raging in Western Europe cast a
threatening shadow across the Soviet Union. Industry and workers
were mobilized for production of weapons.

In June 1940, labor regulations were made more severe. Workers
more than thirty minutes late for work without a medical excuse
lost 25 percent of their monthly wages. Theft of even the smallest
item from a factory, or other misconduct, was punishable by one
year's imprisonment.

The chronic problem of labor drift was dealt with by freezing
workers on their jobs. Whereas workers previously had been *dis-*

couraged from changing jobs by loss of privileges, now they were flatly *forbidden* to do so. An employee required the written permission of the factory management to change his job. If he did so without such permisson, he could be put in jail. A worker who left a factory that manufactured defense items could be sentenced to forced labor for five to eight years.

On June 22, 1941, Nazi armies invaded Russia. For four years the Russians suffered the unremitting agony of war. The Soviet Union's human and material losses in World War II were staggering. The number of dead has been estimated at from seven to eleven million. Some twenty-five million people were made homeless. Factories, power stations, mines, railroad installations, and harbors were obliterated. Thousands of communities were laid waste. About six thousand hospitals and dispensaries were completely destroyed.

The German invaders leveled much of the industry that had been amassed by untold sacrifice. Because of the losses of vast territory and many plants and the recruitment of millions of men into the army, the size of the USSR's labor force dropped sharply during the first few years of the war. In 1943 there were 19,300,000 people listed as workers as compared to 31,200,000 in 1940.

Official statistics show that the labor force recovered in 1945 to 27,200,000 (fewer than the 1940 level, five years earlier) and continued upward to a new high of 33,400,000 in 1948. In 1953, the year of Stalin's death, the total had reached 44,800,000 workers. In 1970 there were about 90 million workers.

As soon as the war was over, Stalin set the exhausted nation to the task of rebuilding. There were new problems to cope with. These were well summarized by Merle Fainsod:

> The mood and temper of the Soviet populace at the end of the war posed serious difficulties for the regime. After the bitter sacrifices of the war, many yearned for peace and quiet, for a relaxation of tempo, and for an opportunity to enjoy the good things of life. Soldiers who served in the West caught a glimpse of capitalist comforts and luxuries which were unavailable in the Soviet Union and transmitted disquieting doubts about the perfection of the Soviet paradise.
>
> Party propagandists and agitators encountered considerable mass apathy when they lectured on political themes. Some members of the intelligentsia displayed disturbing apolitical tendencies. Their openly expressed admiration for Western ideas and artistic models, which was partly tolerated during the honeymoon period of the war alliance, became a dangerous infection as the cold war intensified.[6]

These tendencies were counteracted by traditional methods. As in czarist times, the political police were active. A Russian could not be certain who was a spy and an informer. The man at the next factory bench? The stranger who struck up a casual conversation in a theater lobby? The housewife could only eye with suspicion the other women with whom she shared a common kitchen in a crowded apartment house. Even children were encouraged to tattle on their parents' political views. Russians lived in a state of nervous wariness of fellow Russians. Individuals were driven into social isolation. The arrest of countless citizens suspected of opposition to the regime provided a warning for others.

In this climate of intimidation, rebuilding went forward. The Fourth Five-Year Plan, covering the years from 1946 through 1950, provided a program for the reconstruction and development of the Soviet economy after World War II. From 1946 onward, official Soviet statistics showed a steady climb in industrial production. By 1953, the Russians had not only rebuilt the lost factories, but the country's industrial capacity and output were at record levels far above the high-water mark achieved before World War II. The Russians had again shown their resiliency.

6. Fainsod, *How Russia Is Ruled,* p. 114.

Between 1913 and 1953, Russian industrial production had increased about twenty times. Steel output rose from 5 million tons in 1929 to 41 million in 1954 (still far short of U.S. production where 5,300,000 tons of steel were turned out in 1896 and 42,700,000 tons in 1916).

The Soviet Union found itself not only in the ranks of the world's leading industrial nations; it was now, along with the United States, in the category of a superpower with nuclear capabilities.

Slowly at first, consumer goods began appearing on the market. A correspondent in Russia described what he witnessed in December 1947, when rubber boots suddenly were offered for sale.

> The women's galoshes department in Moscow's mammoth "Mostorg" store was the scene of scrimmage. Women of all ages and conditions, with a sprinkling of men sandwiched in among them, were battling, shoving, and pushing their way toward the counter with a courage and determination worthy of a noble cause. Outside, the police had roped off the entrance and were admitting new customers only one at a time from a line that curled twice around the block. . . .
>
> The run on galoshes continued for a week. Then the authorities stepped in. There was a round-up of speculators who were marketing galoshes in the provinces at several times the legal price. The sale of galoshes in all stores was temporarily suspended.[7]

A half-dozen years later, another correspondent, returning to Moscow from a period at home, reported on the improved availability of goods and on the method of distributing scarce items:

> I allowed myself to be carried by the flow of the crowd into the big GUM store. I was frankly astonished by the variety and wealth of consumer goods which was displayed. The prices were high and quality remained low but in quantity and selection the improvement was obvious. This was especially true in the textiles and dress-goods departments where despite prices which would have put an American housewife into a faint peasants and city women were buying hand over fist.
>
> However, there were still many notable shortages. Only twenty to forty television sets per day were available at prices running up to

7. Edmund Stevens, *This Is Russia Uncensored* (New York, Didier, 1950), p. 40.

two thousand eight hundred rubles ($700 at the official exchange rate) and it was obvious from the queues that there were three hundred to five hundred potential purchasers for each set—maybe a thousand, for such things are hard to judge.[8]

There were more goods, but the cornucopia of comfort remained out of reach of the Russian worker. Stalin's last years were marked by the Cold War, in which suspicion of, and hostility toward, the West gave armament production continued priority over household and personal goods.

There was to be one more purge before Stalin died. In January 1953, an announcement was made that a group of nine doctors had been arrested on charges of plotting against the lives of certain members of the Soviet government. Like ripples on a pond, the circles of suspicion widened; each week brought reports of new arrests throughout the country. The doctors, at the center of the alleged plot, were said to be linked to British and American intelligence networks; the Cold War mentality was evident. There is no better testimony to the fearful atmosphere of the Stalin years than the writings of Stalin's own daughter, Svetlana, who later managed to leave Russia and settle in the United States.

On March 4, 1953, came the announcement that Stalin was dead of a cerebral hemorrhage. It was a common enough cause of death for a man his age. Yet inevitable questions arose. *Was* death by natural causes? Had the doctors' plot in fact existed, and had they *succeeded?* Was the hand of Laurenti Beria, the minister of the interior, involved? He now appeared strong enough to inherit Stalin's power through his control of the vast secret police army. To this day the questions remain unanswered.

8. Salisbury, *op. cit.*, p. 223.

9 The Khrushchev Era, 1953–1964

THERE were at least six potential successors to Stalin, but the front-runner was Beria. It did not take long for the others to join forces temporarily and eliminate him. Within four months after Stalin's death, Beria was arrested and denounced as a traitor by his colleagues, apparently with the support of the army. A special court sentenced Beria to death. On December 24, 1953, it was announced that the execution had been carried out by shooting.

Within a very few years one man emerged supreme from the "committee" government that succeeded Stalin. This was not a surprising development in view of Russia's tradition of one-man rule, but the fate meted out to the losers was unprecedented. The purged men were not executed, imprisoned, or exiled as in the past; they were given jobs of sorts in their fields. For example, Premier Georgi Malenkov, an engineer by training, was assigned to run a power station in a remote region. Foreign Minister V. M. Molotov was sent to Outer Mongolia as ambassador. However demeaning the jobs might be, it was nevertheless a new and civilized way of dealing with defeated political opponents in Russia.

The man who emerged at the top was Nikita Sergeyevich Khrushchev. Head of the Communist party, he had the precise title "First Secretary of the Central Committee of the Communist Party of the USSR." Born on April 17, 1894, in the village of Kalinovka, he joined the party in 1918, shortly after the revolution. Thus he was the first leader of the Soviet Union to have played no role in driving the czars from their throne. A worker in the true sense of the word, he had been employed as a pipe fitter in a coal mine. Once he proudly listed his worker's credentials, telling a visiting delegation that he had "worked at capitalist enterprises, participated in strikes, and negotiated with capitalists." Early photographs show him in typical worker's dress—pants tucked into knee-high boots, long tunic, and military-style cap.

Khrushchev's father had been a shepherd and miner; and, as a child, Nikita had had very little formal education. It was only when he reached the age of twenty-eight that he attended the first of several industrial academies. He rose quickly in the party. For a time he was the Communist chief in the Ukraine, where he loyally served Stalin in an infamous purge of people suspected of opposi-

Khrushchev talking to farmers and workers in the Kustanai Region. *Sovfoto*

tion. An American aid official who knew Khrushchev in the Ukraine recalled that on outdoor occasions he would wear a worker's cap to show his affinity for the proletariat, but the cap was tailor-made and matched his cream-colored linen suit. When he entertained at one of the four houses at his disposal, it was quite regal. Each guest was served individually by a uniformed waiter.

Ebullient, gregarious, loquacious, Khrushchev was a new brand of Soviet ruler. He enjoyed himself at official embassy parties, drinking a formidable number of toasts in vodka, which he held remarkably well. Irrepressible, he engaged in an eye-to-eye debate on the relative merits of communism and capitalism with the then vice-president Richard Nixon, who was visiting the American exhibit at a Moscow Fair. Often crude, he astonished the world and embarrassed his own delegation by taking off a shoe and rapping the table at the United Nations when he objected to a speech. Incautiously outspoken, he engendered suspicion by warning the West that "we will bury you"; in fact, he meant that, by demonstrating its superiority, the Soviet socialist system would outlive the capitalist world.

Khrushchev left a vivid impression on all who met him: "He is one of those roly-poly stout little men—not really fat—who are fast on their feet, almost airy. He leans forward alertly, almost as if he were on tiptoe, when he talks, and his supple mouth is as a rule a tiny bit open, as if his eagerness to devour whatever experience is coming cannot be checked. He has a silver fringe of hair, an upturned nose, three small chins, and twinkling, very dark small eyes set widely apart and deep. It is hard to tell their color—probably deep brown. Two gold teeth shine when he smiles, and a gap is noticeable between the two upper front teeth; he has one mole, or wart, next to his nose in the left cheek, and another under his right eye."[1]

Nothing during Khrushchev's administration surprised the Russians and the outside world quite as much as his attacks on Stalin. A campaign of education and propaganda sought to create a new

1. Gunther, *Inside Russia Today*, p. 100.

image of Stalin in the minds of Russians. He was presented as a villain for the dreadful purges, the forced labor camps, the constant reign of terror. Stalin's contribution to the country's industrialization and to the war victory was denigrated too. Later, some of his reputation in these respects was restored. Since Stalin had been such an all-pervading influence in Soviet life, the program to devalue his importance caused reverberations throughout the Soviet system.

Not the least affected was the Russian worker. The "de-Stalinization" program, as it was called, was to some extent intended to evoke greater production from him. Russia had made great strides; but in the output of meat, milk, and butter, for example, the U.S. still surpassed the USSR by from 50 to 300 percent. Khrushchev announced his intention to overtake the United States in these and other categories.

In a country of still limited resources, everything was then being used to the limit. The new projects and goals conceived by Khrushchev could not be achieved simply by pouring in more resources; all resources were already fully committed—all the resources, that is, but the inner, *human* resources. Exploitation of workers had been the system used exclusively and successfully by Stalin for a long time. Methods appropriate for forcibly raising a nation from a backward agrarian economy no longer achieved the same results once that nation became a technologically advanced industrial power.

Now something was needed other than tightening the grip on Russian workers if Russia's economy was to progress. That something was human initiative, a partial freedom from paralyzing fear, a desire rather than a compulsion to work. The ingredient of consideration for the worker was to be added to the recipe of force.

There was a general moderation of the harsh Soviet way of life. The conversion from the club to the carrot found expression in many ways. Slave-labor camps, which had ceased to pay for themselves in terms of output achieved, were partially emptied and the inmates returned home. Taxes were eliminated on the tiny plots of land that families on collectivized farms were permitted to cultivate privately. Arrest by the midnight knock gave way to more conventional legal forms. Tourists and delegations of farmers, industrialists, teachers, legislators, writers, and workers were admitted from the United States and other countries. Limited numbers of Russians, usually in supervised groups, were allowed to make short trips to the West. Cultural exchanges were started, beginning with an American production of *Porgy and Bess* shown in Moscow and in Leningrad (the new name given to Petrograd after Lenin died); and later the Bolshoi Ballet performed in U.S. cities.

For the Soviet worker, de-Stalinization brought a number of benefits. The forty-eight hour workweek was reduced to forty-six. The extra two hours of free time were taken Saturday afternoon. Enterprises could close earlier on Saturdays by skipping the lunch period that day. A few industries began a seven-hour day and a forty-two hour week, and the hope was to make this shorter week universal.

A minimum-wage law, long taken for granted in capitalist countries, was introduced for the first time in Russia in 1956. The law raised the wage levels of the lowest-paid workers, such as street sweepers and factory watchmen. It provided a minimum monthly wage in towns of 300 rubles ($75). In rural areas the minimum monthly wage was 270 rubles ($67.50). The law exempted persons earning less than 370 rubles ($92.50) from income taxes.

Of greatest significance, the Russian worker was, for the first time, given a legal right to leave a job whenever he wished by giving two-weeks notice. Previously, as has been mentioned, it was an offense, punishable by a jail sentence, for a worker to quit a job without permission. There still were disadvantages to changing one's place of work under the new law: the worker lost his pension accumulation by leaving a job without the consent of the management and would have to start from scratch building his pension fund in a new position.

The Russian worker lacked the right to bargain for higher wages (norms and salaries were still fixed in each industry). There was no unemployment insurance for the job-changer (an average of one month's work and wages are lost when a Russian seeks new

Inside the GUM department store in Moscow. *UNATIONS*

work). But even so, the limited rights granted the workers after Stalin *were* welcome.

Of greatest interest to Russians was the new importance given to the long-neglected production of consumer goods. After Stalin's death, one of the first acts of the government was to declare that a far larger proportion of the country's resources would be devoted to the needs of the buyer. It was explained that heavy industry was in such good shape that new factories could be built to provide a sharp rise in the standard of living. Some existing factories would divert a part of their floor space and man power to the production of consumer items.

When Khrushchev came to power, 70 percent of Russia's productive capability was in heavy industry, including armaments. Only 30 percent was in light industry, including consumer goods. Russia's leaders promised to alter the ratio, increasing the proportion of resources assigned to light industry.

In part, the Soviet leaders were motivated by a desire for popularity. Lacking Stalin's iron grip on the people, they hoped to rally support among workers and others by providing more of the good things of life.

This aim was not quickly attainable. About a year later, for example, an article in *Pravda* on February 11, 1954, reported: "In the great mirrored windows of the Tashkent fashion houses are displayed suits for both men and women, suits fashionable in style and elegantly cut." The newspaper went on to say that the windows are proudly shown to foreign tourists, who are misled to believe that anybody with the money may buy the clothes. "However, at the moment the suits are worn only by dummies in the shop windows. Imagine that you have been bold enough to decide on one of these magnificent creations for yourself. You enter the shop. You are told: 'Alas, we have no suitable material.' If the material should by chance be available you will then be told that they have no lining material, no trimmings. If you overcome this difficulty, you will be asked to bring your own buttons. Along with the buttons it would be as well to bring a tailor. Otherwise you will have to wait a long time for your order."

The unevenness of Russia's economy was evident everywhere. In order to accomplish priority projects, other needs had been neglected. Russia's economy had not been able to produce enough steel and other materials to provide both rockets *and* refrigerators.

At the time that Russia amazed the world by launching its first sputnik on October 4, 1957, it was impossible to buy many ordinary household items in a Moscow store. A worker's wife could not find waxed paper or kitchen aluminum foil. Electric blankets, facial tissues, portable radios were not manufactured. Resources were not invested in air-conditioning units, window screens to keep out flies, or personal deodorants. It *is* possible to live without all of these things. Russians did, and in the case of most of these items, still do.

The contrast between the *two* Russian economies—that devoted to heavy industry and that devoted to consumer production—was striking in the Khrushchev years. The TU-104 was the first jet passenger plane successfully put into commercial service anywhere in the world (except for the British-made Comet, which was grounded after a series of disasters). At Moscow's airport, when the futuristic plane, with its swept-back wings and powerful jet engines, was being readied to receive passengers, attendants trudged aboard bearing old-fashioned teakettles of a design used by grandmother prior to the air age. It was a never-ending source of surprise to watch floors being polished in Soviet office buildings and hotels: a watchman removed one shoe and sock, placed his foot through a strap attached to a brush, and by a jerky, jogging movement, limped along, slowly polishing the floor. Although Russia's technology was obviously capable of producing plug-in electric kettles and automatic floor polishers, the pre-Khrushchev leaders had chosen to divert resources to more vital products.

A montage view of the Russian worker's way of life during the Khrushchev period and into the decade of the 1970s would consist of many diverse elements, often seemingly contradictory. For example, the Russian worker is conscious of the discipline that a police state imposes on him. Yet he shows a total disregard for authority in crossing the streets. Pedestrians surge back and forth whenever there's a momentary gap in traffic, disregarding traffic lights and policemen, who have the authority to impose fines on the spot, but very seldom do. And, oddly enough, Soviet policemen are permitted to smoke while on duty.

The garb of the Russian worker is most often Western in style: pants with wide cuffs, tieless shirt, and jacket. His day-off outfit is an ordinary suit, often rumpled because Soviet-manufactured textiles often do not hold creases well and because dry-cleaning and pressing services are expensive. Women workers may wear overall suits on the job; but off work, skirts and blouses or dresses, often flowered prints, are favored.

Lines are very much a part of the Russian worker's everyday life. There are queues in summer at outdoor stands where soft drinks are sold and in winter in front of stores selling electric heaters. The worker accepts the prevalence of lines as an unavoidable part of daily routine. He respects the queue and seldom tries to edge in ahead of his turn. Yet, in an unorganized crowd, the Russian worker, like other Soviet citizens, is quite undisciplined, rude, even brutal, mercilessly elbowing his or her way, and never pausing to offer apologies.

As much as queues, government regulations are a pervasive factor in the life of the Russian worker. From birth in a government hospital to the grave in a government cemetery, the Russian's life is intertwined with government regulations that reflect a curious intermixture of concern and contempt. Working mothers are granted generous maternity leaves of 112 days with pay, and hospital care is free, but the father is not permitted to see either his wife or baby during their nine days in the hospital. During pregnancy, Russian women are seldom seen on the street. Modesty may be a reason for this, but the unavailability of maternity clothes is a factor; so, without clothes to fit, women usually stay home.

Russian workers—like most of their countrymen—are a robust, warm, emotionally outgoing, generous people, although they smile only when there is a genuine reason. They sacrifice for their children, pamper them, and almost never spank them. Russians love to sing, and their songs are the deep-throated, heart-tugging variety that only a people who have suffered can create. They eat enormous portions of food, heavy on starches and sparse on greens, so

A typical station of the Leningrad subway system, which is a daily part of the Russian workers' routine. *Tass from Sovfoto*

that short, stocky figures are characteristic. The men say they prefer their women to have ample girth.

Russians marry by simply registering their intentions, paying a small fee, and returning a week later to confirm the marriage. No vows are exchanged. In some large cities there is a "Marriage Palace," a government-operated building, where the couple, family members, and friends can participate in a simple ceremony. In some places, though, a district bureau, a small cheerless room with a potted rubber plant in one corner, is the same for registering marriages, births, and deaths. A Communist youth newspaper once suggested that the bride should wear a white or gaily flowered dress for the occasion and the groom should wear a necktie.

Soviet law does not regard a child as "illegitimate" even if the father is unknown. Abortions are legal and free and performed on the woman's request at Soviet hospitals. A state allowance is provided an unmarried mother for her child's care, but the law cannot erase the stigma that many Russians still attribute to unwed motherhood.

The children in a Soviet worker's family go to school six days a week. There is school on Saturday, and Sunday is the only free day. Homework is forbidden on weekends and holidays. Youngsters begin school at the age of seven. Education is compulsory for ten years in cities and for seven years in most villages and farm districts, where schoolrooms and staff have been inadequate. The intention is to make ten-year schooling available nationwide. Some schools are on a two-shift basis. In all grades except the ninth and tenth, children are required to wear uniforms. Girls wear plain brown dresses with big white collars and black aprons. Their hair is almost always worn in long braids, which end in red ribbons tied into bows. Boys wear a military type of uniform with grayish blue pants and high-collared, hip-length tunic gathered in folds at the back by a broad leather belt. The cap is a stiff-visored officers' type; and in the lower grades, at least, boys have their heads shaven.

In the early days after the revolution it was easy to obtain a divorce. During World War II, divorce requirements were tightened, and the divorce act of July 8, 1944, provided that those seeking a divorce must submit to a court hearing and pay a divorce tax of about $30. Divorce in Russia is complicated by the housing shortage. It has not been uncommon for a divorced couple to go on sharing the same room and even the same bed because neither can find another place to live.

The Russian worker pays income taxes, which are higher for the unmarried Russian than for the married Soviet citizen. There is an inheritance tax of about 10 percent, and Russians may make out wills and leave property to heirs.

The Russian worker goes to his grave in an open casket drawn on a hearse while mourners trudge behind in a sorrowful column. The family of the deceased is expected to pay for the coffin, transportation, flowers, and other expenses at the government-operated funeral parlor. Usually the union helps its members bear funeral costs. Needy people can obtain assistance from government social welfare committees in their neighborhoods.

Khrushchev took steps to reorganize Soviet industry. Through the years, control of the country's 200,000 factories and 100,000 construction sites had become concentrated in Moscow. More than fifty ministries directed Soviet production from offices in the capital. Such highly concentrated centralization outgrew efficiency as Soviet industry expanded. It became unwieldy. It took days or weeks for a factory manager in Alma-Ata to receive permission to undertake a simple adjustment in production. One ministry was often isolated from any knowledge of what another ministry was doing. Not uncommonly, this caused expensive overlap of effort. For example, one ministry built a 5,000-ton-capacity iron casting plant in Leningrad even though another ministry was already operating a similar plant nearby with an 8,000-ton surplus of output, which was being shipped to other parts of the country at great cost.

Centralized control could be justified when the Soviet industrial work force numbered 13 million in the early days of Stalin's reign, but it could not cope efficiently with a work force of almost 45 million at the end of Stalin's lifetime. Decentralization transferred much of the initiative from Moscow to the managers in the field.

De-Stalinization and decentralization produced good results in industry. Steel output increased from 4,200,000 tons in 1913 to 51 million tons in 1957; the United States produced 104,500,000 in 1956. The magnitude of growth of Russia's all-important steel output is shown by the fact that in 1913 Britain produced two and a half times more steel than Russia, but that by 1957 the Soviet Union's steel output exceeded the production of Britain, France, and Belgium combined.

From 1913 to 1957, hard coal production rose from 29,100,000 tons to 395 million tons. The corresponding figure for U.S. coal production in 1957 was 479 million tons.

Soviet development, however, was uneven. Some areas as well as industries had been neglected. Two-thirds of the Soviet Union's 78,000 collective farms did not have electricity in 1957. Khrushchev chose to put it another way: "All towns and nearly all industrial settlements and more than one-third of all the collective farms now use electricity." In the same speech Khrushchev admitted that "we have an acute housing shortage" and "we are lagging behind, both in the quantity of the output and particularly in the quality of certain consumer goods, and the cost and prices of these goods still are high."

In one respect, the Khrushchev effort to improve the lot of the workers made no change at all. Women continued to do every sort of work in Russia; they still do today. In 1956, 45 percent of the working force were women. In industry not quite half the workers were women.

Women sweep streets, often with brooms made of twigs; shovel snow; operate cranes; drive buses and steam rollers; dig coal. Women are barbers, lathe operators, bricklayers, judges, and radio announcers. Of Russia's almost 334,000 doctors, 76 percent are women. Seventy percent of Russia's teachers are women. In 1956, about 53 percent of all specialists—persons skilled by reason of higher education in any field of endeavor—were women. One-third of all the deputies elected to regional soviets in 1955 were women. On state farms, 46 percent of the workers were women; in stores and other trading enterprises, 58 percent; in restaurant work, 83 percent; and in health services, 85 percent.

Women work for various reasons. Some admit that low salaries make it essential that they earn wages in order to provide, together with the earnings of the male family members, an adequate income. The official explanation, published in a government pamphlet intended for foreigners, says:

> Our women go to work and are eager to do so, not only because their wage augments the family income, but also because their work gives them economic independence. They work because they want to devote their lives to the common interests of the people, because they want to contribute their own labor to the great construction work being carried on by the Soviet people for the sake of a better life and happiness for their children. Work has become a necessity for the Soviet citizen, for the Soviet woman.

The Khrushchev glove did not entirely cover the historic Soviet mailed fist. In 1957 a law was published to deal harshly with people who evaded work.

Every able-bodied Soviet citizen, whether industrial worker, peasant, or member of the intelligentsia, is expected to work. This has been the case from the time of Lenin and is, in fact, embodied in Marxist doctrine. A Soviet textbook on labor law begins with the following words: " 'Work,' says Engels, is . . . the first fundamental condition of the whole human life; this is true to such an extent that we may in a sense say that work has created man himself.' " Another quotation from Engels is given: ". . . work is the characteristic feature of the human society, distinguishing it from a pack of apes." An article of the Soviet Constitution, a document principally the work of Stalin himself in 1936, contains the same idea: "Work in the USSR is a duty and a matter of honor for every able-bodied citizen, in accordance with the principle: 'He who does not work, neither shall he eat.' "

Yet a certain number of people managed to evade work. Many of these were young Russians whose parents' income made it possible for them to shirk jobs. They lived on "allowances" from their parents, which is scorned in Russia as "unearned income." These youngsters became a target of the 1957 law that provided for deportation to remote regions and compulsory labor in slave-labor camps for beggars, vagrants, and persons living on unearned incomes. The law's preamble declared that socialist society had eliminated unemployment and the exploitation of man by fellow man. It went on: "However, in the industrious Soviet family there still are people leading an antisocial, parasitic way of life. Such people either take up employment for the sake of pretense and actually subsist on an unearned income and enrich themselves at the expense of working people; or, though fit for work, do not do useful work, either in society or in the family, but prefer to engage in vagrancy and begging and often commit crimes."

The law provided that adult able-bodied citizens who shun useful labor may receive sentences of from two to five years of compulsory labor at "a place of deportation." The method of trial for accused persons resembled the procedure of the Salem witch trials. Verdicts were a community responsibility. A simple majority vote at a meeting of adults of neighborhoods, in the case of cities, or of the entire community, in the case of rural areas, would be enough to convict a person. In some instances, a meeting of adult residents of one apartment house, attended by at least one hundred persons, could by a majority vote sentence a fellow resident to a Siberian labor camp. In effect, a handful of Communist party members in a small community could, by taking the lead, sentence an indolent young man to forced labor.

Wages were raised slightly under Khrushchev, but continued to be low by Western standards. At the Likhatchov Auto Works, formerly the Stalin plant (almost without exception, enterprises and places bearing Stalin's name were renamed as a result of de-Stalinization), in Moscow, where forty thousand workers were employed, wages ranged from 750 rubles ($187.50) to 3,000 rubles ($750) a month.

Executives received more. Ivan Ivanovich Karsov, assistant director of the plant, for example, was paid a monthly salary of 5,000 rubles ($1,250) besides bonuses. In a good year, when the plant overfulfilled its production targets, Karsov's bonus could increase his salary by 50 percent or more. A short, balding man with searching brown eyes, he was at the top of the Soviet industrial wage scale; but his was not an exceptional salary, by Western standards, for the vice-director of the nation's largest vehicle factory.

There are advantages other than salary, though, for a man in Karsov's position. He had a chauffeured car assigned for the use of his family. In a country where money alone cannot purchase adequate living space, Karsov's position entitled him to a large apartment for his wife and three children. As is true of almost all Russians in top managerial positions, Karsov was a member of the Communist party, the thin layer of populace that runs the country. His party membership and managerial status gave him the prestige, influence, and respect that often accompany wealth in capitalist countries.

Karsov typified the successful Russian worker who rose to a position of importance in Soviet society. More important than his considerable ability in the automotive field was his loyal service in the Communist party ranks. Born in 1907, Karsov was only ten years old at the time of the revolution. He began working at the plant as an apprentice in 1921, three years before it produced its first motor vehicle. It was then a repair shop. He learned a machinist's trade, was sent to an automobile institute, and graduated in 1935 with a rudimentary knowledge of engineering and plant management.

He was admitted to the Communist party in 1930, having participated earlier in Communist youth organizations. In 1939 he was part of a group sent to the United States to purchase machinery for the plant; large sums of money were involved and he spent two years there, inspecting the performance of machinery before returning to Russia. He visited a number of American auto plants and observed the assembly-line techniques. Many of the U.S.-built machines bought by Karsov are still in use and the name "Cincinnati" stands out incongruously on pressing machines and lathes near walls decorated with posters of Lenin and "Increase Production" slogans in the Cyrillic alphabet. There were also large machine tools made in Germany, France, and England. In recent years, replacement parts for these are being made in the Soviet Union; and almost all new machines, except for those from Communist Czechoslovakia and East Germany, are manufactured in the USSR.

Karsov's responsibilities were extensive. Besides running the plant, the management was concerned with housing projects, schools, and nurseries for employees' children. There were two polyclinics on the premises where minor injuries and ailments were treated, and more complicated ills received attention at the plant's hospital. The plant employed 124 doctors and 184 nurses. Two thousand youngsters of plant employees attended sixteen kindergartens. Six thousand employees belonged to twenty-nine sections of the plant's "Torpedo" sports club. Technical schools run by the plant were attended by more than a thousand workers.

The Likhatchov factory operated its own health resort on the Baltic Sea, where the best workers and privileged persons like Karsov and his family were able to obtain reservations. There was also a smaller rest home for vacationing employees about fifty miles from Moscow. Tickets to other government-operated rest homes were sold to deserving workers, but by Karsov's own figures, only 8,500 workers of this plant's 40,000 were able to obtain tickets for any of these vacation spots in any one year.

The plant had a large recreation building, called a Palace of Culture, whose gymnasium was used for Communist party lectures as often as for basketball games and whose auditorium was the scene of as many classes as movies.

Each year the plant had built six hundred apartments for its workers. This is another factor to dissuade people from leaving their jobs. There is a law—enacted in the Khrushchev era—that an occupant of an apartment may not be evicted for going to work in another job, but pressures from neighbors can serve as well as a law to force a family out. The construction work was done by one thousand builders in the employment of the plant, but the financing of the construction was by government funds, and it is the government that actually owns the apartments. The factory's role is to supervise their construction, assign their occupants, and manage them when completed.

Distribution of apartments is on the basis of "a complex of factors," to borrow Karsov's phrase: a worker's seniority, the number of members in his family, and the condition of his present flat. Assignment of flats is made by the management, the Communist party unit in the factory, and the union.

Although the factory bears the name "auto works," very few *cars* were produced. The assembly lines—working on two shifts—concentrated on trucks and bicycles. Both are vehicles of labor in Russia. In villages and on farms the bicycle is not a vehicle of sport or recreation, but rather an important means of carrying people to and from work. The plant produced 450,000 bicycles, 100,000 trucks, and 3,000 buses annually. A bicycle was completed every minute; a truck, every five minutes; a bus, every two hours; and a refrigerator, every ten minutes. Karsov said that "several hundred Zil limousines" are manufactured each year. The Zil, standing for the initials of the plant, is made only for the use of the Kremlin leaders and other government organizations. The Zil closely resembles the pre-World War II Packard in its long lines and pointed front. Asked about this, Karsov replied, rather evasively and with a trace of embarrassment, it seemed, that "with the development of auto techniques, all cars look very much alike. After all, if you build a car it looks like a car. With the exception of some midget cars, all cars look like American cars. There's nothing unusual in the appearance of the Zil as many details will be the same in *all* cars."

Although selling prices varied with the purchaser (prices for sales abroad depend on the foreign-policy considerations of the transactions), the average charges for products of the Zil plant were: 15,000 rubles ($3,750) for the several models of dump trucks, 40,000 rubles ($10,000) for buses, 70,000 rubles ($17,500) for the seven-passenger Zil car, and 600 rubles ($150) for a bicycle. The Zil refrigerator, white-enameled with two ice-cube trays and a small freezer compartment, sold for 2,000 rubles ($500) and worked reliably. Except for some expansion, little has changed at the factory in recent years, and the conditions described during the Khrushchev era are typical of most big Soviet factories today.

Nikita Khrushchev's success in improving the worker's conditions was not matched in all of his other undertakings. He invested great numbers of men and women and huge amounts of money in trying to grow abundant harvests in low-rainfall areas of Siberia and Central Asia. The results were marginal. Relations with Communist China degenerated during his period in office. One product of de-Stalinization was to generate a spirit of independence in the Communist countries of Eastern Europe, the so-called "Soviet satellites." There was a revolution in Hungary, which Soviet tanks repressed; revolt in Poland was narrowly avoided only when Russia made concessions.

All of this created critics and personal enemies for Khrushchev. His unpolished personal style in diplomacy was held partly responsible for Soviet foreign-policy setbacks. In October 1964, while Khrushchev was out of town, his opponents sensed that the time was favorable to hold a vote in the Presidium of the Communist Party to oust him as first secretary. They assured themselves that the composition of the much larger Central Committee of the Communist Party would sustain the Presidium's decision. It did. Khrushchev was out.

Most remarkable was that this was accomplished by a vote and without trials or executions or other bloodshed. Political and personal intrigue was involved, but nothing more sinister. The precedent Khrushchev had set at the beginning of his term saved his life at the end. Khrushchev was given a *dacha* (country house) twenty-five miles from Moscow, an apartment in town, a car and chauffeur. He was rarely seen in public, and then usually to cast his vote for the single slate of Communist party candidates at elections. He never spoke out publicly on politics. Khrushchev knew better than anyone the unwritten rules of the new game. One of these rules was that a "retired" Soviet leader must keep his grievances to himself. On September 11, 1971, Khrushchev died of natural causes. He was buried without official ceremony or recognition for his achievements on behalf of the workers and other Soviet citizens.

10 The Russian Worker Today

FROM the time of the czars, we have seen that a period of liberalization in Russia has generally been followed by a period of tightened control. It was thus expectable that the pendulum would start to swing again after Nikita Khrushchev's relatively benevolent rule.

A process that has come to be known as "re-Stalinization" took place. This does not mean that the purges and mass exterminations that characterized Stalin's rule were repeated. What occurred was less extreme. Worker discipline was hardened. Higher priority was given to heavy industry over consumer production, and there were more shortages of goods in stores than before. Authors who wrote critically of the Soviet system were exiled to Siberian prison camps.

Instead of speaking of "peaceful co-existence with the West" and "peaceful economic competition with capitalism," as had Khrushchev, the new leadership in its early days urged "a sharpening of the international class struggle." In 1968, when Czechoslovakia under Alexander Dubcek experimented with "socialism with a human face," which included freedom of speech and the press, Soviet armies invaded that country.

Russia's leaders acted from a sense of insecurity and inquietude. Khrushchev's de-Stalinization program may have awakened dormant productive energies in Russian workers, but it also had ignited a spirit that threatened authority, not only in the USSR, but in Eastern Europe as well. Beyond the Soviet Union's eastern frontiers, China, with several times Russia's population, was acting hostilely; and there were border skirmishes with casualties on both sides.

The instinctive reaction to all of this on the part of Khrushchev's successors was to retreat from permissiveness on all fronts. The new leaders reacted as they did because that was the way they were trained; they lacked the individuality and breadth of spirit that enabled Khrushchev to act differently. "The present leaders started for the most part in humble posts in the newly Stalinized party of the early thirties, whose main activity (particularly in the Ukraine) was an almost unbelievable brutal crushing of the peasantry. Most of them made their careers in the great purge of 1936–38, a period when the qualifications required for promotion were denunciation of one's comrades and servility to the Stalin machine."[1]

The two top men who succeeded Khrushchev had spent part of their lives as factory workers and managers and could be taken as exemplars of how far a worker of simple origins can climb in the USSR. Neither they nor others in the ruling Presidium could be described as "big" or "imposing" personalities. Most of the new rulers had been junior associates of Stalin, and the Soviet writer Alexander Solzhenitsyn suggested that "while Stalin would not tolerate failure, he also hated it if people were too efficient . . . so Stalin's touch turned everything into mediocrity." Another writer described the sequence of leaders from Lenin onward as "a rapidly plunging graph."

Leonid Brezhnev took over as head of the Communist party and emerged as the most powerful leader. He had become a party

1. Robert Conquest, "Stalin's Successors," in *Foreign Affairs*, April 1970.

member in the Ukraine in 1931, while a student at a metallurgical institute. He played a role even then in enforcing Stalin's collectivization of the peasants, which, it will be recalled, resulted in millions of deaths. Completing his education, he was given a managerial post in a factory in 1935 and was able to hold on to it during the terrible purges of that period, when many factory executives were among those eliminated on vague suspicions of disloyalty. In 1937 he was promoted to a position equivalent to that of assistant mayor of Kiev, the capital of the Ukraine. He moved up fast and in 1950 was appointed to the top post in the Communist party in Moldavia, a so-called republic noted for a particularly uncompromising manner of party rule. In 1952, Stalin brought Brezhnev to Moscow and appointed him to the Central Committee of the USSR Communist Party.

The second most important figure among Khrushchev's successors was Alexei Kosygin, who became prime minister. In 1935, upon graduating from the Leningrad Textile Institute, he became a foreman in a textile plant. He played a role in a city-district party committee, when the main activity has been described as "the denunciation and purge" of previous party officials. An opening left by the purges provided the opportunity for Kosygin to be appointed director of Leningrad's enormous October Textile Works. He advanced to become the mayor of Leningrad and caught Stalin's eye as early as 1939, when he was brought into the sphere of national party activity.

The post-Khrushchev period found the Russian worker restive, weary of waiting for the promised plenty to materialize in his daily life. The new Soviet leaders were aware of the needs and aspirations of the ever more literate, sophisticated Russian worker. In 1967 the workweek in most industries was reduced to forty hours —a five-day week with Saturday and Sunday off. In 1969 wages were increased for most workers by an average 3.9 percent. Yet there have been very few significant improvements in terms of a richer existence and greater personal liberty.

At the outset of their administration, Brezhnev and Kosygin made promises of industrial and agricultural reform that would improve living standards. But these promises were soon doomed when the new leaders felt compelled to renew emphasis on military production. Fears of China, commitments to the Arabs in the Middle East, the trauma of Czechoslovakia—these factors determined the allocation of resources. It was a replay of the old story—insufficient means with which to provide both guns *and* butter. It has been conservatively estimated that 60 percent of Soviet industry works directly for the military at the expense of the Russians' living standards.

In 1971, with relative stability restored within the Communist empire and relations with the West improving, the Soviet leaders moved toward satisfying consumer yearnings. The Ninth Five-Year Plan (1971–75) laid stress on raising living standards and swelling the supply of consumer goods. It was the first five-year plan to schedule a greater increase in output from consumer industries than from heavy industry. Among other things, this meant that a certain proportion of Soviet resources that might otherwise go into military production would now go into peaceful manufacture.

It was, in part, the desire—or perhaps the necessity—to reduce military expenditures that caused the Soviet leaders to sign the historic treaty limiting nuclear arms deployment, along with other agreements, during President Nixon's trip to Moscow in May 1972. It was the pressures from workers and other citizens for improved living conditions that helped motivate the Soviet leaders to conclude the subsequent trade agreements with the U.S.A.

The living standard of the Russian worker remains well below that of the worker in the United States and in West European countries. However, the concept of "the standard of living" does not lend itself easily to measurement. As Soviet specialist Keith Bush has pointed out in a comparative study of living standards, "It means different things to different people. For some, it is simply the quantity and quality of consumer goods and services available or, in other words, the degree of material well-being of a community. . . . Most of us would choose to add other, less easily quantifiable, aspects of the 'quality of life' such as education, health, welfare, employment opportunities, working conditions, leisure facilities, the freedom of religion, speech and travel, environmental factors and so on . . . [For example], the fear of being ill and thereby incurring crippling medical bills seems to be peculiar to the U.S. middle class citizen and not, generally speaking, to his Soviet or West European counterpart [who feels secure through government insurance plans]. The ability to walk in a nearby park at any time without any danger of being mugged or molested is, for most of us, a more desirable 'consumer good' than, say, the ownership of a deep-freeze or color-television."[2] The Soviet workingman and his family lack the deep-freeze and color TV, but can walk without risk in their parks.

Another way of gauging relative living standards is in terms of the amount of time a worker must spend at his job to earn sufficient money to buy certain products. The following table does that:[3]

WORKING TIME REQUIRED TO BUY SELECTED FOOD AND CLOTHING ITEMS IN NEW YORK CITY AND MOSCOW, JULY 1, 1970

	New York	*Moscow*
White bread (1 pound)	5.4 minutes	17 minutes
Butter (salted, 1 pound)	16.4 minutes	140 minutes
Beef (rib roast, 1 pound)	18.7 minutes	62.6 minutes
Potatoes (1 pound)	2.1 minutes	3.9 minutes
Milk (1 quart)	5.6 minutes	24 minutes
Eggs (1 dozen)	12.2 minutes	92.6 minutes
Sugar (1 pound)	2.5 minutes	40.3 minutes
Soap (toilet, 1 bar)	2.0 minutes	16.3 minutes
Vodka (1 fifth) . . . . 1 hour, 36 minutes		6.6 hours
Cigarettes (1 pack)	8.5 minutes	15.1 minutes
Street dress (women's, man-made fibers) 5.6 hours		42 hours
Stockings (nylon)	17.5 minutes	2.9 hours
Shoes (women's leather)	5.3 hours	33 hours
Suit (men's woolen)	26.3 hours	157 hours
Shirt (men's cotton)	1.7 hours	11.4 hours
Shoes (men's leather)	6.0 hours	35 hours

2. Keith Bush, *Indicators of Living Standards in the USSR and the West* (Radio Liberty Research Paper, June 4, 1970).

3. Edmund Nash, "Purchasing Power of Workers in the Soviet Union," in *Monthly Labor Review*, May 1971 (U.S. Department of Labor, Bureau of Labor Statistics).

Many Russians buy their everyday needs from street vendors, such as the one tending this corner fruit stand in Moscow. *UNATIONS*

Although Soviet salaries are low, many families do have substantial incomes simply because every member of the family works. Take the example of the Sergeyev family. The mother is a doctor earning the ruble equivalent of $212.50 a month. The father is a fabric designer in a textile organization and earns $325. A son works as a translator and makes $550. A younger daughter is a student in an institute, where her monthly stipend from the government contributes nothing to the family income, but covers a few of her personal needs for food, movies, and an occasional dress. With a total family income of almost $1,090 each month, the Sergeyevs pay only $10 per month rent for their two rooms. By pooling their income, the Sergeyev family purchased a television set for $550, the father buys a suit once a year for $317.50, and they can afford to eat out in restaurants occasionally.

With each passing year, the Soviet citizen seems increasingly conscious of his living standards. He wants improvements. It has

been said that the Soviet Union is in the grip of a new revolution—
a consumer revolution, a revolution that the leaders can no longer
ignore and that can no longer be appeased by appeals for more
sacrifices for communism.

Greater contact with the Western world has made most Russian
workers keenly aware that their standard of living lags far behind
the capitalist world. According to estimates in 1972, the average
monthly take-home pay of a Soviet industrial worker was $127,
compared to $529 for his American equivalent. The West German
counterpart earned $307, and the British, $253. The disparity
existed, too, when the prices of a standard food basket of twenty-
eight items were compared. It would have cost $56 in Moscow,
compared with $33 in New York, $48 in Munich, and $38 in
London. Other comparative statistics convey the same picture:

> Though the Soviet population exceeds that of the U.S. by nearly 40
> million, four times as many people own television sets in America as
> in Russia. And in color television: Russia last year [1971] produced
> its first 60,000 color sets and is aiming at an output of 200,000 this
> year. That compares with more than 41.5 million color sets owned in
> the U.S.
>
> For every Russian family that owns a refrigerator there are eight
> American families that own one. Home freezers, commonplace in the
> United States, are not even produced for private use in the Soviet
> Union. . . .[4]

To retain perspective with regard to all of the preceding statistics, one should take into account that, for the Soviet worker,
medical care, education, and often vacations are free. Rent is very
cheap, seldom more than 5 percent of the salary of the head of the
family; electricity and other utility charges are often only double
that modest figure. The Russian worker in the 1970s can buy a
wider selection of clothing than ever before and can eat plentifully,
even if the fare is plain. Most Soviet workers have enough money
left over after the purchase of essentials to save up for a television
set, a movie camera, a refrigerator, even a car. Although the country's housing shortage remains acute, the waiting lists for apart-

4. *U.S. News & World Report*, May 15, 1972, p. 30.

ments in the vast new residential complexes on the outskirts of major cities have grown shorter.

An American correspondent noted some other improvements:

A few years back, the Soviet housewife who wanted to feed her family had no choice but to stand in line in a half dozen different food lines each day. Within the last two years, however, several Western-style supermarkets have been built in major Soviet cities and hundreds of smaller self-service grocery stores have opened.

Only a couple of years back, ordinary toilet paper was a chronic "deficit good," despite the almost limitless supply of pulp in the rich Russian forests. Now Russians can even buy paper towels.

In central Asia, shoppers can buy the local equivalent of an American barbecue grill; a butane-fueled shish kebab cooker. The Soviet Ministry of Light Industry turns out hundreds of items to meet the demands of Soviet workers with leisure time on their hands—everything from sleeping bags to outboard motors. . . .

The quantity and selection of goods have grown rapidly, but the quality, on the whole, is still the shoddiest in Europe. There are more goods on the shelves, but service personnel are probably the rudest in the world.[5]

Crowded housing is one of Russia's main domestic problems. Few things preoccupy the Russian worker more. It is not at all uncommon for four persons to live in a single room, which serves as parlor, dining room, and bedroom. When Moscow was in the throes of an Asian flu epidemic, doctors published recommendations on how to prevent spread of the disease. Isolation was suggested. In the conditions of Soviet housing, no more effective isolation could be provided than simply hanging up a sheet to separate the flu sufferer's bed from those of the other members of the family.

Government regulations state how much space each person is entitled to as a minimum. For Moscow, each inhabitant is supposed to be assured of nine square yards of floor space—that is an area measuring three yards by three yards; but even this guarantee is not always fulfilled. The housing shortage encourages a novel kind of house-hunting:

5. Dean Mills, *Baltimore Sun*, May 19, 1972.

Apartment "switching" is common all over the Soviet Union. Newly married couples in Moscow, each with a room of their own, try to find a couple with a two-room flat who are getting divorced, so that they can trade their accomodations. Illegal brokers arrange these deals, for fees of hundreds of rubles.[6]

There is extensive construction of massive apartment buildings going on in most Soviet cities. The visitor driving into Moscow or Leningrad or Kiev or Tashkent from the airport sees scores of ten-story apartment houses, some completed, others still under construction. The scale of the projects is impressive; but the needs are enormous, not only to keep up with normal population growth, but also to replace dwellings destroyed in World War II, to permit families sharing space to obtain separate quarters, and to replace old buildings that become uninhabitable through age.

The situation was well summed up by Nikita Khrushchev in a speech on the fortieth anniversary of the Bolshevik Revolution:

We have an acute housing shortage. The reasons for this are understandable. First, Soviet power inherited an incredible housing shortage from the old order. Second, in Soviet years the population in towns and workers' settlements has increased more than three and a half times. Third, in the prewar years we were compelled to economize on everything, including the construction of dwellings, so as to be able to put every kopeck into heavy industry. Fourth, tremendous damage was caused to dwellings during the war which left nearly twenty-five million people without a roof over their heads.[7]

Foreigners are seldom invited to the home of a worker or any other Russian. Long indoctrination in suspicion of Westerners is one reason; even though a Russian may not *believe* the indoctrination, he realizes that it is best not to court official suspicion by defying it. Another potent reason is that many Russians are ashamed to show their crowded quarters.

The home of a factory foreman in Rubtsovsk, Siberia, was shown to a visiting American because it was lavish by Soviet standards. On the third floor of a five-story building lacking an elevator, it

6. Robert G. Kaiser and Dan Morgan, *Washington Post*, December 19, 1972, p. A-20.
7. *Tass*, November 7, 1957.

consisted of a living room, a bedroom, and private kitchen and bathroom. The toilet had no flush mechanism, but the bowl could be removed to be emptied. The bedroom contained two beds for the mother, father, and youngest child. An elder daughter slept on a bed in the living room which, in the Russian custom, held a jungle of rubber plants and other space-consuming greenery. The beds were the customary Russian iron bedsteads with a thin mattress and two great, overstuffed pillows at the head, covered by bridal lace. The counterpane of lace, an umbrella-sized orange or yellow lampshade, and spreading plants are inevitable decorative features of Soviet apartments.

Most new apartments of the type available to fortunate Soviet workers consist of three-room units—one family to each room. There's a common hallway for coat racks. From this hallway opens a door to each family's room and other doors to the communal kitchen and bath. Older apartments have six, eight, or even a dozen families sharing common premises.

To facilitate cleanliness under these crowded conditions, there are public bathhouses in most neighborhoods. Overcrowding discourages large families, although the government encourages a high birth rate.

The poor workmanship of Soviet apartment-house construction strikes foreigners and is, in fact, often a subject for criticism by Soviet newspapers. Precious steel is used sparingly, if at all, in the construction of apartments. That is one reason why new buildings quickly look old; the lack of steel reinforcement causes sagging, cracks in the plaster, and doors that won't close properly.

Vacations offer Russians an opportunity to escape briefly from their crowded homes. Russian workers are guaranteed vacation time by law (in most cases from two to four weeks, depending on the length of time a worker has been employed in an enterprise). Shortly after the revolution, in 1919, Lenin decreed that all confiscated mansions and palaces of the czars and nobility in favorable locations be converted into vacation resorts for the workers. "Sanitoria" and "rest homes" are the rather unenticing official designations for such places. For example, the Livadia Palace, the imperial family's summer residence mentioned in Chapter 3 as the place where Czar Alexander III died, is now a vacation sanitorium for workers afflicted by minor respiratory and lung ailments.

Tickets are given to outstanding workers to spend their vacations at the government resorts. These are much in demand because hotels (also government-owned, of course) at holiday sites are few and expensive. The distribution of resort tickets is the responsibility of trade union officials. From time to time criticism of these officials has been published for assigning the limited number of tickets to themselves and their families rather than to deserving workers.

At Livadia the all-inclusive price for a month's stay is the ruble equivalent of $350, but most of this amount is covered by the free trade-union ticket. The main mansion and its outlying buildings consist of sixty-eight rooms and, with dormitory sleeping (even on vacation), can accommodate 750 guests. The staff is large—550 maids, waiters, waitresses, and cooks and fifty-four doctors. The large room where the famous Yalta Conference took place during World War II is now a dining room. The room that once held the czar's billiard tables is a large communal bathroom.

Although three thousand sanitoria and rest homes have been built by the Communists, these are not nearly enough to satisfy the needs of the people. Many workers are unable to obtain the required trade-union tickets, and there have been cases reported of speculation—tickets sold illegally by a recipient at a profit. Even though Russian families are usually close-knit, a husband and wife often go on vacation separately. The reasons are several: since often both work, their vacations may not coincide; also it may be impossible for both to obtain tickets for the same resort.

Besides vacation time, there are four annual holidays for the Soviet worker—the Revolution Anniversary on November 7; Constitution Day on May 5; May Day on May 1; and New Year's Day. With two days off on both November 7 and May 1, the total number of work-free days is six.

In this day and age private ownership of cars must enter into the consideration of the worker's life-style in any country. The Soviet

The assembly line at the Volzhsky automobile plant, built under the supervision of the Fiat Company in Togliatti. The new cars are called *Zhigulis*. *Novosti from Sovfoto*

Union's *total* output of cars in 1971 was only 529,000. This compares with the production in the United States of about 9 million cars and close to 2 million trucks (about 550,000 trucks were produced in the USSR).

In 1970 there existed in *all* of Russia about two million cars; this same number of privately owned vehicles is registered in the Paris region alone. The dream of many Russians, oblivious to the disadvantages of traffic congestion, is to possess an automobile. Russians in every city and town have placed their names on waiting lists for new and used automobiles. In Moscow the list was closed to additional applicants when forty-two thousand names were inscribed. A person who had succeeded in getting his name on the list could expect to wait two to four years before actually getting a car. Car ownership brings its problems: during the long, bitter Russian winter most private owners are forced to store their automobiles under canvas because of a shortage of antifreeze and winter oil.

The individual Russian's prospects of driving his own car improved slightly, but only slightly, toward the end of 1970. At that time, the first few models of Fiat automobiles came off an assembly line in a factory built under the supervision of the Italian company. Despite Russia's advanced state of industrial development, Moscow had turned to the West for technological assistance in car-building, a field in which Soviet experience was comparatively limited. Almost all the machinery in the Fiat plant is Western-made.

During the first year of operation, the factory was geared to produce 20,000 small, four-door sedans, a modified version of the Fiat-124 model. The plant was designed eventually to reach a capacity of 660,000 cars annually.

The Fiat, like other cars produced in the USSR, is out of the price range of most workers and of Russians in general. It carried a ruble tag amounting to $6,100—equivalent to more than four years' wages for the average Russian worker. The same car sold in Italy for about $2,000.

Russia had a long way to go to enter the automotive age in other respects as well. A news magazine summarized the situation:

> As yet, the Russians have not even begun to think about drive-ins, roadside restaurants or other conveniences that are a part of the auto age in the West. In Moscow alone, a city of seven million three hundred thousand, there are only nineteen repair shops, one hundred and five gas stations and thirty-two parking lots. "When I need my car fixed, I have to call a plumber," laments one Moscow auto owner. . . .
>
> Since the housing shortage places a higher priority on new apartments, virtually no garages have been built. Cars must be kept outside. . . .
>
> Roads are generally narrow, often pass directly through small villages, and have broken surfaces. They are a major cause of Russia's alarmingly high accident rate.[8]

A Moscow weekly, *Economic Gazette*, commented on the ridiculously low auto speed attainable on cross-country travels, estimating the average as eighteen miles per hour and adding: "Our great-grandfathers traveled by troika from St. Petersburg to Moscow at about the same speed two hundred years ago." The *Gazette* also

8. *Time*, September 21, 1970.

noted that the chemical industry has failed to come up with a paint for marking road lanes that does not fade almost as soon as it is applied.

History, it has often been said, has a way of repeating itself; and nowhere is this more true than in the USSR. Many of the complaints against workers publicized in Lenin's time, and again in Stalin's and Khrushchev's, are preoccupying Soviet authorities of the present era. Speaking at the Kharkov Tractor Plant on April 13, 1970, Brezhnev said:

> There are many instances of valuable working time being wasted, of people being late for work, absent from work without a valid excuse, and loafing about sometimes through being drunk. I shall not conceal the fact that we receive letters in which workers, collective farmers, and engineers propose an intensified struggle against those who disorganize production and against loafers, drunkards and work-dodgers. I believe that this is a very proper demand. We should not be lenient toward people who are to blame for serious damage to our society, for wrecking the fulfillment of plans by enterprises and shops, and causing conscientious workers to lose wages.[9]

Great attention is paid to the problems of drunkenness and alcoholism. In the past, campaigns against these evils have stressed that drunkenness leads to hooliganism, crime, and the breaking up of families. In recent times the emphasis is on drunkenness as an economic crime leading to absenteeism and production delays. One factory in Tomsk was reported to have lost 2,300 working days in one year through absenteeism caused by drunkenness.

Khrushchev's attempt to increase production through greater freedom and a degree of capitalist-style, materialist incentive has given way to the more traditional Communist methods of so-called "socialist competition" and exhortation. It was not by mere chance that Alexei Stakhanov, the miner who gave his name to the movement to increase work norms (discussed in Chapter 8), was suddenly lifted from obscurity in September 1970; he was given one of Russia's top honors by being made a "Hero of Socialist Labor."

9. *Tass,* April 13, 1970.

Sixty-five years old at that time and an assistant engineer at a mining enterprise, Stakhanov received the award for "great services in the development of mass socialist competition." Similarly, the 1919 practice of the *subbotnik* (mentioned in Chapter 7), a Saturday worked without pay, was resurrected on April 11, 1970, in celebration of the centenary of Lenin's birth. Workers throughout the country gave up a free Saturday to labor without pay as they had done almost half a century earlier, when the Soviet state was just struggling into existence.

In spite of a plethora of setbacks and perennial difficulties, the Russian worker has made enormous strides through the years. He has built a powerful industrial machine. His own welfare has steadily, although slowly, improved. Critics of the Soviet Union and its Communist system often argue that the workingman's condition would be incalculably better had czarism and some form of capitalism survived. It is futile to argue the question because it is a hypothetical one.

It is also profitless to try to draw comparisons between the Soviet and the American worker on the basis of relative freedoms. As has been seen from the outset of this book, the Russian worker has *never* had a taste of the freedoms taken for granted in the West. The Russian in the first factory under Peter the Great lacked the right to strike, and that right has been withheld under the Soviet leaders. Freedom of speech was as *unknown* under the czars as it is today. The right of collective bargaining did not exist in the time of the empire, and it does not exist now. These and others are not freedoms *lost;* they are freedoms never attained. This distinction is fundamental in the attitudes of the Russian and Western workers toward freedom.

Even so, it is hard to escape the conclusion that the Russian worker has achieved painfully less in terms of goods and services, in terms of comforts and luxuries, than his efforts and the resources of his country would seem to have promised. Many explanations can be offered in terms of economic theory and history (especially the country's devastation in wars), but one consideration in particular should not be overlooked. That is that the Communist

The very old and the very new exist simultaneously in present-day Moscow. (*Foreground*) the Kremlin, built during the time of the czars; (*background*) modern apartment and office buildings. *Tass from Sovfoto*

system has failed to achieve the maximum from the Soviet worker and from Soviet resources because it has tried to repeal an immutable law of human nature.

This law is that the human worker requires rewards to produce to his fullest capacity. He needs incentives. He is materialistic. He is acquisitive.

This is not to deny man's more spiritual and idealistic motivations. A worker may be spurred to great effort by a sense of duty or patriotism, or by the sheer satisfaction from a job well done. But, basically speaking, although man may not live by bread *alone*, he cannot live *without* bread; and he produces best when butter, jam, clothes, housing, cars, and so forth are attainable along with the bread as the *direct* rewards of his efforts.

In a sense, the Soviet leaders have recognized this. They say that a "new Soviet man" is being created who is motivated entirely by *community* interests rather than by individual greed. Idealistic and desirable as this may be, the "new Soviet man" has not yet evolved nor is there any reason to believe he will.

Lacking the incentives and rewards of the capitalistic system (whatever the many evils of the capitalistic system may be), the Soviet worker has failed to match the productive accomplishments of the worker in the West.

This does not mean that the Soviet worker is a disgruntled and disloyal person. Far from it. There are many Russians dissatisfied because of shortages, crowded housing, red-tape bureaucracy, lack of freedoms. But dissatisfied Russians talk about *changes*, about improvements, not about revolution. Most Russian workers seem convinced that their system is preferable to all others and that in time they will achieve, in their own way, the advantages they now lack. And it is just as well that the Russian worker has this optimistic attitude, since he has no tangible reasons for anticipating fundamental changes in his way of life in the near future.

Bibliography

Barry, Herbert. *Russia in 1870*. London: Wyman and Sons, 1871.

Brailsford, Henry Noel. *The Russian Workers' Republic*. New York: Harper, 1921.

Brandes, Georg. *Impressions of Russia*. New York: Thomas Y. Crowell, 1966; reprinted from 1889.

Bruford, Walter Horace. *Chekhov and His Russia, A Sociological Study*. New York: Oxford University Press, 1947.

Burroughs, Harry E. *Tale of a Vanished Land, Memories of a Childhood in Old Russia*. New York: Houghton Mifflin, 1930.

Bury, Herbert. *Russian Life Today*. London: A. R. Mowbray, 1915.

Carrington, George. *Behind the Scenes in Russia*. London: George Bell and Sons, 1874.

Charques, R. D. *A Short History of Russia*. New York: E. P. Dutton, 1956.

Churchill, Winston S. *The Aftermath*. London: Macmillan, 1941.

Crankshaw, Edward. *Cracks in the Kremlin Wall*. New York: Viking, 1952.

Dicey, Edward. *A Month in Russia, During the Marriage of the Czarevitch*. London: Macmillan, 1867.

Fainsod, Merle. *How Russia Is Ruled.* Cambridge, Mass.: Harvard University Press, 1953.

Field, Mark G. *Doctor and Patient in Soviet Russia.* Cambridge, Mass.: Harvard University Press, 1957.

Fischer, Louis. *Russia Revisited, A New Look at Russia and Her Satellites.* New York: Doubleday, 1957.

Gilliard, Pierre. *Thirteen Years at the Russian Court.* New York: Doran, 1921.

Gunther, John. *Inside Russia Today.* New York: Harper, 1957.

Kelly, David. "The Psychology of the Soviet Soldier," from B. H. Liddell Hart, ed., *The Red Army.* New York: Harcourt, Brace, 1956.

Kerensky, Alexander. *The Crucifixion of Liberty.* New York: Day, 1934.

Léderrey, Ernest. "The Red Army During the Civil War," from B. H. Liddell Hart, ed., *The Red Army.* New York: Harcourt, Brace, 1956.

Levine, Irving R. *Main Street, U.S.S.R.* New York: Doubleday, 1959.

Levine, Irving R. *Travel Guide to Russia.* New York: Doubleday, 1960.

Massie, Robert K. *Nicholas and Alexandra.* New York: Atheneum, 1967.

Pares, Sir Bernard. *A History of Russia.* New York: Alfred A. Knopf, 1953.

Payne, Robert. *The Life and Death of Lenin.* New York: Simon and Schuster, 1964.

Salisbury, Harrison. *American in Russia.* New York: Harper, 1955.

Schwartz, Harry. *Russia's Soviet Economy.* New York: Prentice Hall, 1954.

Silver, Boris. *The Russian Workers' Own Story.* London: George Allen and Unwin, 1938.

Stevens, Edmund. *This Is Russia Uncensored.* New York: Didier, 1950.

Tugan-Baranovsky, M. I. *The Russian Factory in the Past and Present.* St. Petersburg, 1898.

Turin, S. P. *From Peter the Great to Lenin.* London: Frank Cass, 1968.

Youssoupoff, Felix. *Lost Splendor.* Translated from the French by Ann Green and Nicholas Katkoff. New York: G. P. Putnam, 1953.

Index